SOBER
MAGIC

SOBER MAGIC

USING THE TAROT AND RITUAL IN YOUR JOURNEY AWAY FROM DRINKING

SARAH POTTER

RUNNING PRESS
PHILADELPHIA

Running Press
Hachette Book Group
1290 Avenue of the Americas, New York, NY 10104
www.runningpress.com
@Running_Press

First Edition: December 2025

Published by Running Press, an imprint of Hachette Book Group, Inc.
The Running Press name and logo are trademarks of Hachette Book Group, Inc.

The Hachette Speakers Bureau provides a wide range of authors for
speaking events. To find out more, go to www.hachettespeakersbureau.com
or email HachetteSpeakers@hbgusa.com.

Running Press books may be purchased in bulk for business, educational, or
promotional use. For more information, please contact your local bookseller or the
Hachette Book Group Special Markets Department at Special.Markets@hbgusa.com.

The publisher is not responsible for websites (or their
content) that are not owned by the publisher.

Print book cover design by Tanvi Baghele
Print book interior design by Sara Puppala

Library of Congress Cataloging-in-Publication Data has been applied for.

ISBNs: 979-8-89414-071-1 (paperback), 979-8-89414-072-8 (ebook)

Printed in United States of America

LSC-C

Printing 1, 2025

To my grandmother, Corrinne,

with endless love and gratitude

for your wisdom, guidance, and

unwavering belief in my magic.

You are in everything I do.

CONTENTS

THE FOOL'S
SOBER JOURNEY

1. **THE FOOL**: I choose to set out on the path of sobriety, a new beginning filled with new opportunities and endless potential.

2. **THE MAGICIAN AND THE HIGH PRIESTESS**: By embracing a belief in magic, I know that everything is connected and I am never alone.

3. **THE EMPRESS AND THE EMPEROR**: By nurturing myself, I make empowered decisions.

4. **THE HIEROPHANT AND THE LOVERS**: Through self-reflection, I gain an understanding of my true nature and uncover the parts of myself to accept and release with love.

5. **THE CHARIOT AND STRENGTH**: By committing to radical honesty with myself, I find my true fortitude and continue to move forward on my path.

6. **THE HERMIT AND WHEEL OF FORTUNE**: Self-acceptance through self-discovery supports my invocation of change.

7. **JUSTICE AND THE HANGED MAN**: Humbly asking for help offers a new perspective.

8. **DEATH AND TEMPERANCE**: I am patient with myself as I invoke my personal transformation.

9. **THE DEVIL AND THE TOWER**: Committing to making major changes by righting my wrongs, I find freedom.

10. **THE STAR AND THE MOON**: A deep commitment to self-reflection and honesty allows me to see my wrongs and promptly right them.

11. **THE SUN AND JUDGEMENT**: My higher purpose provides a guiding light on my divine path.

12. **THE WORLD**: My journey of spiritual awakening is never complete because there is always more to discover through the lessons of practicing sober magic in all my endeavors.

INTRODUCTION

"She fainted!"

Who fainted? I thought as I began to look around the room and focus my gaze. Shoes featured prominently in my line of vision. *Oh no. It was me. I was the one who fainted.*

I was lying on the floor of the nightclub, a position I had found myself in so many times before, in nightclubs and bars in countless cities. Blacking out had been a near nightly experience when I was drinking.

But what caused me to faint this time? I hadn't blacked out in years. Did I slip up? Where was I, and how did I get here? I struggled to gather my thoughts and figure out the context preceding this blackout. Time did not exist in that moment; I was suspended in confusion.

As I fumbled around for some semblance of context and clarity, I checked in with each of my senses just like my therapist had taught me to do when I felt overwhelmed either by anxiety or psychic energy. As I tuned in to the sensations on my skin, the taste of the lime in my mouth from the water I had been sipping, and the bright lights piercing the darkness, I realized I was not drunk and felt immediate relief.

As I tried to focus, I made eye contact with a familiar face—a woman I recognized because she had loved my long-ago boyfriend's band. Ten or so years earlier, she'd gone to all of their shows, and I vividly remembered her watching me on more than one occasion as I rummaged in my purse for loose ADHD pills, illegally obtained, which I would proceed to throw for my then-boyfriend to catch in his mouth or crush up into lines on the greenroom table to snort. Once she'd even seen me tumble down a flight of stairs onto a stage where the band waited, so inebriated I could barely walk. She'd never seemed to like me much, but maybe that was because I wasn't at my best when out of my mind with alcohol and pills. Now, having just watched me pass out yet again, she'd certainly never believe I'd gotten clean and sober. It's hard to be perceived clearly by someone who only knew the old you, the you who was at your lowest. It was such a strange coincidence, seeing her again in this moment—one more sign that something weird was going on psychically that night—and I was suddenly gripped by the feeling that I'd never escape my old self.

That's when the shame really hit me. I didn't want to be viewed as the drunk girl who blacked out. I'd been that girl for far too long, and this humiliation sent me right back to a different time in my life. I closed my eyes again, and when I fully came to, I could hear the familiar voice of my friend James, whose band was supposed to be playing tonight. He was frantically explaining to a looming security guard that I was most certainly not under the influence of any substances.

"Man, just tell me: What did she take?" the security guard pressed. "And do you know how much?"

"I keep telling you, she's not on anything! She wouldn't take anything. She's just . . . she's *psychic!*"

I kind of wished James had just said I was high. It was a better explanation than the truth. How do you tell strangers that you passed out in a bar not because of the excessive drinking and drugs that used to take you down regularly, but because you were overwhelmed by a spirit in the building that had made it clear you shouldn't be there, which you ignored? And then there was the knowledge of the bartender stealing money, the glasses that were about to shatter because another bartender was grieving the loss of her relationship and not paying attention, the second register's till that was short by $5.32, *this* person's dead uncle who had a message, and the fact that *this* girl was cheating on her boyfriend with *this* guy . . . I'd just been hit with so many visions at once my mind had short-circuited. Who would ever believe that? In this moment of disorientation and panic, I was afraid the truth would earn me laughs at best or a psychiatric hold at worst.

My body felt immensely weak, but I started to sit up. I wished I could just disappear. This was supposed to be my friend's big comeback concert, but instead, I was pulling all the attention.

"I'm OK. I just forgot to eat today," I lied. I'd used this line before to cloak my secret in normalcy.

"We are going to get you out of here," the security guard told me, and as if on cue, a young EMT came rushing over with a wheelchair.

I was mortified. This seemed like far too much for a silly little psychic blackout, even if I really needed it—I'm so psychically sensitive that when I get hit with too many visions at once or even do too many readings in succession, sometimes I become so weak I can barely walk until I've rested for a few hours.

As I was being wheeled out of this overstimulating music venue, I had been sober for five years, eight months, and six days. That was also how long it had been since the last time I'd blacked out and come to with no understanding of what had happened. Here I was, frantically making sure I hadn't lost any of my belongings in the fall—just like I used to do all the time. But then I thought: *Used to, but not anymore,* and I realized I was OK. I was more grateful than ever for my sobriety, grateful that I was in control and wasn't drinking.

Still, I *did* collapse; I should have known better than to ignore the energetic red flags.

The signs had been very clear. Even as I walked up to the nightclub, I could feel in every fiber of my being it was not a place I should go into. There were spirits there that didn't want to be seen, as can often be the case with venues—music and drinking both encourage spirit activity, as do the excess electricity from amps and lights and the high volumes of people coming in and out; it's like a never-ending loop. I've seen a lot of wild encounters in music venues because people don't know how to clean or clear the energy, no one's negotiating with the spirits, and a lot of unhinged stuff is going unchecked. On this particular night, it was all coming together to scream: *We don't want you to see what we're up to, so you'd better get out of here!*

I'd ignored a hard warning like this once before, at a museum on the site of an old estate home in California where I'd been brought in to act as a medium. The spirit of that house, who happened to be the original owner, did *not* want me to go into one particular room, and when I did, I instantly fainted.

Even though my abilities limit me in some ways, I can be stubborn. I want to be *normal*, whatever that is. Don't we all? I don't really understand why I see and feel what I do, but there are threads of healing ability and intuition that run through my family and I've been communicating with spirits since I was a small child—it's the only reality I have ever known. Even so, at times like this, it still felt challenging to navigate.

I just wanted to have a regular Friday night seeing a friend's band play a show, not receiving cosmic messages from beyond. Everyone wants time off, even a psychic. But I am so sensitive, I rarely have any downtime, and when I betray my intuition and energetic boundaries, it has harmful effects. Is it any surprise that I took to drinking and getting high to dull my senses for a time?

As we got outside, the EMT was trying to reassure me, "You probably just breathed in an excess of carbon dioxide and that's what caused you to pass out."

I sighed. "Actually, I know exactly what happened," I explained. "And I want to apologize because I totally lied and I hate lying. I did eat today—I ate a lot before I got here because I had a vision I would pass out. I know it sounds unbelievable, but it's true." I decided I didn't have anything to lose and went on, "See, I'm a psychic medium, and this place is so haunted."

The EMT was sputtering as the security guard laughed and rolled his eyes.

"The bands must be so freaked out when they experience the energy in there," I continued. "Feeling drunk even if they haven't been drinking. Their personal belongings going missing and turning up in the most unexpected places. And what is up with register two always being short?"

"You haven't said anything I haven't heard before," the security guard said. "Can I see your ID?"

As I was searching for it, the spirit of an intense older woman suddenly began chattering at me with messages.

"Why isn't my boy cooking?" she asked me repeatedly with increasing intensity.

I looked up from my bag and fixed my eyes on the security guard. "Were you close with your grandma?"

He looked at me skeptically but nodded.

"Grandma Patty?" I asked.

He nodded again.

I don't usually do this, especially not so publicly, but I was in a weakened state and her personality was too strong to ignore. Spirits visit the people they care about who are still living, and this one wasn't going to stop putting pressure on me until I passed on her message.

"Well, she's quite a powerhouse. She keeps asking me why her boy isn't cooking. So, what's up? Why aren't you cooking?"

Suddenly, the security guard was crying. I wasn't surprised. Everyone cries, then apologizes for crying, even though tears never make me uncomfortable.

"I'm sorry," he said. "It's just . . . my dream was to be a chef, and my grandmother is the one who put me through culinary school. She died a few years ago. But cooking for a living just doesn't seem practical, so I'm enrolling in the police academy this fall. Is she mad at me?"

She was annoyed, she told me. She'd made sacrifices to send him to school. I recognized the emotion immediately, the irritation that comes from seeing the potential in someone you love that they refuse to embrace on their own.

I didn't want to say all of that. I receive so many messages within messages, and I do my best to sift out what comes through as the most important ones. The pushy relatives with vibrant personalities always come through more easily, and in this case, she thought she knew better than he did. I think that's something many of us can relate to when it comes to dealing with a loved one who only wants what's best for us. The dead really can be just like the living! I bet she'd been just as forceful when she was alive. In my experience, spirits are the same on the other side as they were when they were here.

"She isn't mad at you, and she isn't disappointed in you, either," I told him. "Our loved ones who have passed look out for us. Your grandma loves you and believes in you, and she wants you to be happy. Life is for the living, and you get to do what you want to do, regardless of what your grandmother wants for you. We are the ones here on Earth. Just do what makes you happy. But whenever you do find yourself in the kitchen, you should know that she's in there cooking with you."

The security guard wiped away his tears and thanked me. He told me I could stay and watch the show if I wanted, but I really needed to get out of there and rest. As beautiful as it can be to receive and deliver messages like that one, it's also exhausting, and I need to take care of myself to do this work I love and be of service.

The level of sensitivity I experience every day is my normal, and the clarity of sobriety has helped me love and accept myself as I am and understand what I need for my own self-care. I had completely forgotten what it was like to black out, but fainting that night reminded me how I used to feel so many nights as I was drinking and getting high. I cannot believe *that* was ever part of my normal. Sobriety has shown me that it doesn't have to be—and that drawing boundaries around my energy is essential.

Like many sober people, my journey was unexpected and both entirely my own and yet totally predictable. A lot of people who live the way I do—who experience emotions so deeply, who are so finely tuned to the energy around them, who are supremely sensitive—have difficulty understanding how to navigate the world. Getting sober can feel like tarot's Tower card: an earth-shattering, radical change that burns everything you once knew to be true to the ground. It's not easy to navigate that kind of upheaval.

I know that I've been able to stay sober for this long and do the real inner work that I've done because of my dedication to a spiritual path guided by witchcraft and tarot. These modalities have supported my commitment to sobriety in a way that nothing else could, and they have quite literally saved my life. Through this work, I have learned how to love and accept myself and radiate that love and acceptance out to the Universe. I have learned that the part of myself I tried hardest to bury—my immense sensitivity—is actually the superpower that has allowed me to find my higher purpose and live a beautiful and satisfying life supporting people through their hardships and helping them love themselves.

I wrote this book to share what I did that worked for me. I hope these experiences, stories, tarot spreads, and rituals can become part of your tool kit to help you embrace your beautiful sensitive nature and understand yourself, too. Perhaps, in the past, you've turned to alcohol or other substances to soften the energy of the world, and perhaps that worked for you until it didn't. That was my situation, and I learned that while those coping mechanisms never really were what was best for me, tarot and witchcraft are.

Rather than numbing me, tarot and witchcraft empower me to feel comfortable in my skin and fully present in every situation by tuning me in to what really matters. They have helped me find my way back to my power, and I hope they can do that for you as well. Maybe you have found this book because you are questioning your relationship to alcohol— whether as an addiction or not—because you sense you need to reassess your triggers and challenges and face them without a numbing veil of substances. This book is for you as well. Witchcraft often appeals to those of us who have felt othered and are looking to explore and enhance our personal sense of power. A pursuit of magic and an interest in the occult are often outlets for those who have a high level of empathy. It's understandable to need extra support if you are feeling everything so deeply, and the tips in this book are for you.

In the numerical sequence of the tarot's Major Arcana cards charting the Fool's Journey from naive new beginnings to the triumphant closure of the World, the fiery destruction of the Tower is followed by the healing waters of the Star. The key to making sobriety work is not just eliminating substances from your life: it's showering your soul with the brightest light and giving yourself space to be present and feel and reflect in order to uncover *why* you were checking out. Once you learn strategies to identify triggers and cope with stress and couple that with newly structured routines and better habits, it's far easier to enjoy your new lifestyle without relying on substances.

I think tarot is one of the greatest tools for storytelling. My practice with the cards has helped me understand my own story of where I was coming from, where I was in the moment, and where I wanted to go. Ritual helped me create structure and routine in my life. This book is the story of my first year of sobriety and the rituals and tarot spreads I used to navigate my own Fool's Journey back to myself and a place of connection to my intuition with my heart open to the possibilities of diving into the unknown with a willingness to change.

The foundations of recovery I use here are based on the traditional twelve steps, which I have reframed through the lens of tarot. Each step is paired with tarot cards from the Major and Minor Arcana and illustrated through insights as I let go of my old life and identity and stepped into the power of a proud witch and tarot reader.

I encourage you to read this book accompanied by a tarot deck of your choice. Pull out the cards that correspond to each chapter, and keep them on your altar or somewhere you can see them as you dive into the lessons of the step. Each chapter includes tarot spreads to further embody the steps and enable greater understanding, as well as simple rituals to do anywhere, most of which require only candles and basic ingredients that are likely already in your kitchen.

Sobriety, witchcraft, and tarot saved my life, and they can help yours, too. Let's go on a Fool's Journey through the cards and the steps together. And remember—as always—to take what you need and leave the rest.

THE FOOL

✧ ✧ ✧

I CHOOSE TO SET OUT ON THE PATH OF
SOBRIETY, A NEW BEGINNING FILLED WITH NEW
OPPORTUNITIES AND ENDLESS POTENTIAL.

✧ ✧ ✧

Tarot's Major Arcana begins and ends with the Fool.

The Major Arcana cards take us on a metaphorical journey through life's mysteries, lessons, and experiences, offering opportunities for growth and transformation along the way. That journey represents our symbolic exploration of the unknown, with endless potential for self-discovery.

The Fool's Journey feels uncannily like the journey I have embarked upon living substance-free in the clarity of sobriety. That journey has taken me into the depths of my own Underworld to discover why I do the things I do, uncover and dismantle deeply rooted patterns, and ascend to the light on the other side of the darkest shadows with greater understanding, loving acceptance, and insight to transform and change what is within my power.

Sobriety has taught me that when we begin anything new, especially something that brings a major change like the challenges of living substance-free, we are inherently the Fool. But we must not forget that there is a full deck of cards to come as well: we may be the Fool now, but we are also every card in the deck at different moments! There are always new lessons to learn, perspectives to discover, and changes to invoke. Life is long, and I think it's quite satisfying that we don't know everything and there are always opportunities to admire the world with wonder and dive into the unknown. In that way, it's wonderful to be the Fool!

I urge you to keep that in mind as you begin your own journey, wherever you hope it will take you, and embrace the unknown rather than turning from it in fear—even though I know as well as anyone just how difficult that can be.

When I finally realized I needed to get sober, it felt like everything was unraveling, but that wasn't the first time I'd felt that way. I had known for years that something wasn't right, but it was easier to pretend than to face what real change might mean. I'd confide in various boyfriends, admit that I thought I had a problem with drinking. And every single one said the same thing: that I wouldn't be fun anymore if I stopped. And I believed them. Being fun had always felt like a part of who I was, despite my shyness, and I felt like that aspect was when I was drinking. Would getting sober mean losing that? Would I be boring? Would people still want me around? I wasn't ready to let go of that version of myself. I didn't know who I'd be without it.

It took a real low point for me to finally get serious about sobriety. I felt like my life was in shambles when another romantic relationship ended; I was running my own business and trying to keep up in the rapidly changing art world; and I had then-undiagnosed PTSD after being violently attacked by a man. Basically, I was running from my feelings—but we all know running away from problems never resolves them: it just makes them worse.

Admitting you have a problem is the first step, but I didn't want to let anyone know how bad things had gotten. I didn't want to admit it even to *myself.* I felt like I was at the bottom of the deepest darkest pit and the only way out was somehow clawing my way toward the light. When things fully fell apart, that was when I realized I needed to change *everything*—and I was finally ready.

I moved back in with my parents outside New York City for starters. It had become clear to me that I needed to learn how to take care of myself. The coping mechanisms I had developed on my own just weren't working: I had no structure, no routine, and no rules, and I was in desperate need of an anchor. My problems seemed so immense that I didn't know where to begin. But starting and ending each day with *something* felt like it could be a first step toward creating a routine. Anything more than that was too overwhelming to contemplate. When an artist I was working with sent me a copy of a tarot deck he'd created, I realized that tarot could be the tool I needed in that moment.

I have always been drawn to the magical and mystical, and I'd developed an interest in tarot at a young age. It began when I was twelve and picked up my first deck at the mall. I had questions about the boy I had a crush on (of course), and the Magician on the box looked as though he knew all the answers. I began trying to memorize the cards and read for my friends. But I got into trouble soon after for offering readings for a dollar in gym class, and after being teased for being a witch, I also wanted to be viewed as "normal." So I resolved only to consult the cards in secret. Eventually, my connection to the cards dwindled until I barely picked them up at all.

But in the stillness of the Hudson Valley at my parents' house again, free of substances and chaos for the first time in a very long while, I was able to think about what brought me joy—an emotion I honestly thought I might never experience again. I don't think it's a coincidence that when I needed it the most, my friend's deck arrived. It made me realize how badly I'd missed reading tarot, and it felt like a divine sign.

I decided I would pull a card each day to reconnect to my intuition. One card at a time, one day at a time. While I desperately wanted to get sober for real and stick with it, I still had no idea how to establish a routine. But this small step of getting reacquainted with tarot guided the way, and I started to have a little more structure in my life simply through pulling a card every morning, contemplating its meaning, and writing my thoughts in my journal.

Here are the cards I pulled those first five days—my earliest days of sobriety:

DAY ONE: TEMPERANCE

Sometimes, the cards are just so uncanny. The first one I pulled was Temperance, the Major Arcana card that is all about moderation, the ability to not dip into extremes, and, yes, sobriety. I researched Temperance in my various tarot books and favorite blogs to see what insight I could find. "Balance. Harmony. Patience. Serenity."—I felt a complete lack of all of these. Stillness made me excruciatingly uncomfortable, and I hated to wait. I wanted everything yesterday, and if it took any longer than that, I searched for ways to speed everything along. This felt like an impossible lesson to learn, but I wrote it all down in my journal before getting myself to my noon AA meeting.

That meeting began with the Serenity Prayer: "God, grant me the serenity to accept the things I cannot change, the courage to change the things I can, and the wisdom to know the difference."

Something about saying *God* like that always freaked me out, but this time it faded into the background so that I could hear the rest of the words more clearly. May I have the *serenity* to accept the things I cannot change. May I have the *courage* to change the things I can. As a self-proclaimed control freak, I knew this would be a big ask.

Before going to sleep, I sat with the Temperance card again and transcribed the Serenity Prayer underneath my morning notes. "I want to accept the things I cannot change. I want the courage to change the things I can. Will I ever understand the difference?"

The Temperance card gave me hope that maybe one day I could.

DAY TWO: THE EMPEROR

On the second day, I pulled the Emperor, a paternal card that reminds us of the power of routine and order. "Authority. Discipline. Control. Structure."—I wrote these words in my journal and tried to sit with the disgust I felt around what they meant to me. The idea of structure and routine made me bristle because it felt like a cage: something built to contain me or strip away the wildness that made me feel alive. Routine felt boring and limiting, but the revulsion was my mind's way of attempting to protect me from the rigid rules and fear I'd once endured. Trauma teaches the nervous system to associate consistency with control so even neutral or helpful structure can feel like a threat until safety is slowly, lovingly rebuilt from within.

I had always wanted to take a yoga class, and that seemed like a good way to achieve some Emperor energy. The only class I could find that day was light stretching and long poses for senior citizens in a neighboring town. It was pay what you wish, though, which was all I could afford. That felt like a cosmic yes from the Universe, so I went.

I was by far the youngest in the room, but everyone welcomed me warmly. It was a struggle to sit in the stillness of my body, but it did feel good to just focus on stretching and balancing instead of the myriad anxieties and questions that usually filled my mind. Before I left, the instructor pulled me aside and mentioned that they met on Tuesdays, Thursdays, and Saturdays and she hoped I would be back. I did, too.

In my journal that night, I wrote, "Knowing where you need to be and when could be a good thing. It's nice to have something you can count on. PS: Try setting alarms so you actually get to places on time."

DAY THREE: DEATH

This pull felt visceral. I wrote in my journal: "Change. Transition. Transformation. Endings. If I am really going to be sober, everything has to change, and there is so much I am going to have to give up."

DAY FOUR: THE EMPRESS REVERSED

The mother figure of the Major Arcana arrives to nurture, but when she appears reversed, she reminds us to tend to our own needs and make self-care a priority. I wrote "SELF-CARE" in all caps in my journal and underlined it three times.

In yoga class, we focused on our breath and being present. The instructor's final words echoed in my mind as I held my knees to my chest in Apanasana: "Balance and focus are necessities. Listen to what your body is telling you. You are important, so take the time to nurture your mind, body, and spirit."

Before bed, I got out the Empress card again and looked over the imagery more intently. She lounged confidently yet comfortably on her throne with a direct, knowing gaze. Her gown was covered in pomegranates, my favorite fruit, and a twelve-star crown sat atop her head. A heart-shaped shield with the symbol of Venus lay at her feet, and the background was lush with trees and wheat and sunshine. She looked so serene yet so empowered, a feeling I realized I would love to invoke for myself. I wrote a little more in my journal:

"I still don't know what self-care is exactly, but the Universe is clearly telling me I need to figure it out. It's nice to do nice things for myself, and my day felt easier when I actually gave myself the space to be on time and enjoy myself. Remember this: you are important so take the time to nurture your mind, body, and spirit."

DAY FIVE: TEMPERANCE

Temperance again. Was this some sort of cosmic joke from the Universe, taunting me to stay sober with a constant reminder that I had a problem with indulgence and struggled with moderation?

I continued my daily card pull throughout the first year of my sobriety and beyond. Even if I accomplished nothing else, I knew I could count on my tarot time in bed. I started putting my morning card on my altar so I could continue to contemplate it throughout the day. By keeping a tarot journal, I began to see the patterns. This practice helped me get to know myself, strengthen my intuition, and recognize where I needed extra support in my sober journey.

I'd like to invite you to try this, too. Even though it may seem small, committing to any daily routine is an important act of self-care. This time in the morning is yours—a gift you are giving yourself—so you should treat it accordingly. If we simply stop drinking or numbing out but don't examine why we did any of that in the first place, it can be challenging to shift our relationship with alcohol and stay substance-free for any significant period. That's why I think it's so helpful to create time and space to be thoughtful and considerate of our emotions.

Let's pull a card. Hold your deck in your hands, close your eyes, and take a few deep breaths in through your nose and out through your mouth. Now begin to shuffle your cards, whatever way feels best for you. As you shuffle, ask yourself, your higher power, the Universe:

What do I need to know to be guided through this day?

Or:

How can I best support my recovery today?

Hold the energy of your question, and when you feel ready, choose a card. Look carefully at the illustration and notice all the tiny details. What does this card mean to you? How does it make you feel? Are you intrigued? Are you put off? Are there characters in the scene depicted on the card? What are they doing? What are their facial expressions and postures telling you? Your initial impressions of the card are the first steps toward your answer. There is no right or wrong here, so let your intuition guide you.

After spending a few minutes intuiting the guidance from the card's imagery, write down some notes in a journal you've picked out specifically for your daily tarot card pull. Check in with the guidebook that came with your deck, and any other tarot books you like, and see what the author has to say about your chosen card. Did you pick up the same messages or something else completely? How has their interpretation enhanced or affected the message coming through to you? Is there anything you now see about the card you had not noticed before? Put all of this down in your journal as well, and then get moving into the rest of your day.

In early recovery, you may find yourself pulling a lot of Major Arcana cards since this is the portion of the deck referring to monumental lessons and seismic shifts. Now, with more years of understanding and a better perspective, I see my early card pulls of Temperance as a reminder that the Universe had my back and was supporting me through my struggles rather than laughing at me or challenging me or any other negative interpretation I had at the time. There are no good or bad cards in the deck, just lessons and moments to consider as helpful advice.

Before you go to bed, create some time and space to consider what you learned from your card that day, even if it was nothing at all. Write a few notes down about how the card manifested throughout the day.

You can always return to this tarot journal for additional advice and support through your card pulls. I like to think of my journal as emblematic of the Magician card. In a typical depiction of the Magician, the figure is seen standing by a table that displays a sword, a wand, a pentacle, and a cup—the symbols of all four Minor Arcana suits—to remind us that the Magician is the ultimate manifester who can make anything happen because they possess all the tools to do so. This journal is one of *your* tools to make anything and everything happen in your sobriety. But remember: we can only be the empowered Magician because we've also been the Fool taking that first step on the journey.

THE FOOL AND STEP ONE

— ◇ —

Admission of Powerlessness, Openness to New Experiences, Taking a Leap of Faith, Childlike Trust and Humility, Facing the Unknown

The Fool is associated with new beginnings, innocence, spontaneity, and a sense of adventure. In relation to sobriety—particularly step one of recovery, where we acknowledge and admit our powerlessness over addiction and recognize where life has become unmanageable—the Fool card has several meaningful connections to consider. Just as the Fool embarks on a journey without knowing what lies ahead, individuals in recovery are taking a courageous step toward a new life. There is often an abundance of uncertainty, but that doesn't need to overshadow that this is also a hopeful moment full of potential.

The Fool represents a fresh start and the ability to leave behind past burdens, and acknowledging the need for change is central to step one. When we admit we have a problem, even if in that moment we feel boxed in by our current circumstances, we are creating space for limitless potential. And if you can dance on that summit with the Fool and jump off the edge into a new way of being, life is guaranteed to be different from here on out.

In recovery, confronting the unknown of a future without substances can be daunting, but it is essential to move forward without being weighed down by the past. This relinquishing of fear can lead to empowerment and healing. Step one requires a leap of faith—while acknowledging that support will be needed along the way.

The Fool's new beginnings, trust, and spontaneity resonate deeply with the first step of recovery. We can acknowledge our challenges—our powerlessness and our unmanageable lives—and at the same time set out on a new journey toward healing and personal transformation.

THE ACES OF THE MINOR ARCANA

— ✧ —

Step one is all about surrendering control, admitting powerlessness over addiction or destructive patterns, and opening the door to a new way of living. The Aces represent beginnings, gifts, and divine invitations, each one offering a unique facet of spiritual awakening that aligns with the essence of step one.

Ace of Wands
INSPIRATION, DESIRE, AWAKENING; THE SPARK OF WILLINGNESS

This is the spark, the first flicker of willingness. It represents the desire for change and the inner fire that ignites when we admit we can't keep living the way we have been. The Ace of Wands is the soul's call to action, the readiness to try something different—even if we don't know exactly what it will look like yet. It's hope.

Ace of Cups
HEALING, OPENNESS, EMOTIONAL RENEWAL; READINESS TO FEEL

This card represents emotional surrender. The Ace of Cups is the willingness to feel again, to soften, to be vulnerable, and to allow love (including self-love) to start trickling back in. In step one, it's the recognition that shutting off our emotions hasn't protected us—it's isolated us. This card is the first tear, the first prayer, the first moment of connection.

Ace of Swords
TRUTH, CLARITY, BREAKTHROUGH;
RADICAL HONESTY

This is the mental clarity that often comes after a long period of denial or distortion. It cuts through illusions and invites radical honesty—the kind that step one demands. The Ace of Swords is the breakthrough thought, the brave admission, the decision to speak the truth: "I am powerless, and my life has become unmanageable."

Ace of Pentacles
STABILITY, OPPORTUNITY, COMMITMENT;
THE BEGINNING OF A GROUNDED
PATH FORWARD

This is the physical commitment to doing things differently. It could be the first meeting, the first sober day, the first time we reach out for help. It reminds us that recovery isn't just emotional or spiritual; it's grounded in tangible choices. The Ace of Pentacles holds the promise of a new, abundant life, one small step at a time.

⌒⎯☀⎯⌒

Together, the Aces mirror the wholeness of step one. They hold the fire of desire (Wands), the heart of surrender (Cups), the mind of honesty (Swords), and the grounded action of commitment (Pentacles). Step one isn't just an ending; it's the beginning of a sacred, magical rebirth.

A TAROT SPREAD TO EMBARK ON YOUR OWN FOOL'S JOURNEY

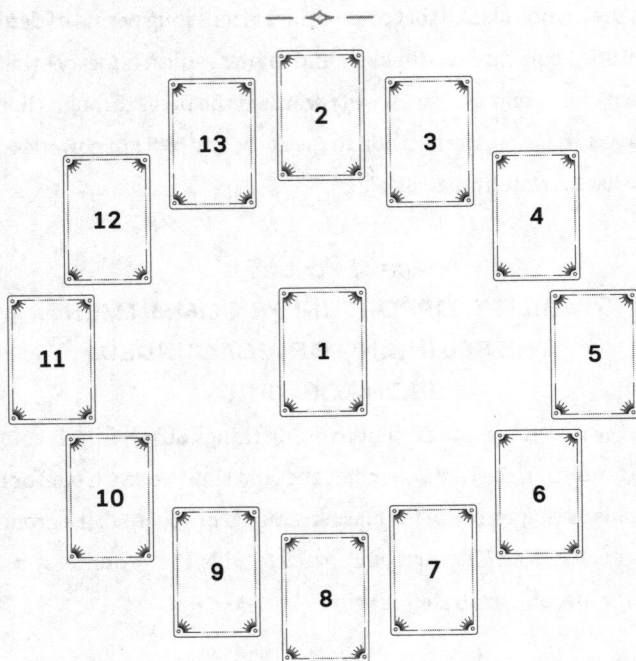

— ◇ —

```
         ┌─────┐  ┌─────┐  ┌─────┐
         │     │  │     │  │     │
         │ 13  │  │  2  │  │  3  │
         └─────┘  └─────┘  └─────┘
┌─────┐                          ┌─────┐
│     │                          │     │
│ 12  │                          │  4  │
└─────┘                          └─────┘
┌─────┐        ┌─────┐           ┌─────┐
│     │        │     │           │     │
│ 11  │        │  1  │           │  5  │
└─────┘        └─────┘           └─────┘
┌─────┐                          ┌─────┐
│     │                          │     │
│ 10  │                          │  6  │
└─────┘                          └─────┘
         ┌─────┐  ┌─────┐  ┌─────┐
         │     │  │     │  │     │
         │  9  │  │  8  │  │  7  │
         └─────┘  └─────┘  └─────┘
```

Whether you are embarking on your maiden voyage with the Fool or you have traveled the path many times over, there is always something new to discover! Allow the energy of the Fool to inspire you to boldly move into the unknown.

For Card 1, ask: *What aspect of the Fool will I embody this year? What is the major lesson the Fool will teach me in this round of our journey together?* Think of this as the overall theme of your year ahead in sobriety to anchor your practice.

This card provides insight on where to place your focus this year. This is something the Universe knows you are ready to face. Maybe it's caring for your physical health and mental well-being, or maybe it's focusing on your financial stability or diving more deeply into your romantic relationship patterns. Whatever it is, allow it to shift as the year progresses so you may embrace the lessons with flexibility. Sometimes we might expect one thing but be surprised by something else entirely. Allow these lessons to delight you rather than intimidate you!

Pull twelve more cards. Each one offers insight into the details of the energetic theme for the corresponding month in the year ahead. This is your road map of the possibilities and potential for your personal Fool's Journey through sobriety over the coming months! I think it's very important to balance the notion of being present through the ideal of one step at a time while also creating structure, tools, and thoughtful points to consider.

A TAROT SPREAD TO ILLUMINATE FEELINGS AND CREATE A STRATEGY

— ◇ —

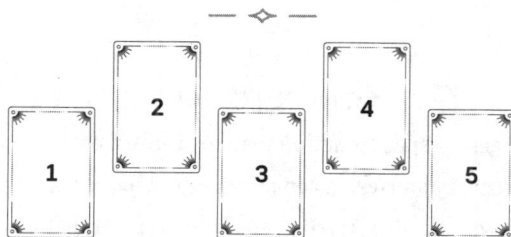

The Fool's themes of new beginnings, courage, and trust align well with the foundational principles of step one in recovery. The energy encourages newly sober individuals to embrace their journey, recognize their potential for change, and move forward with an open heart and mind. In keeping with that goal, this tarot spread is tailored to support understanding and embodying these principles to illuminate your feelings and strategies on the path ahead.

Card 1
CURRENT EMOTIONAL STATE

This card represents where you currently stand emotionally and psychologically in your recovery journey. It can reveal your feelings about addiction or substance use and the challenges you face in diving into sobriety.

Card 2
ACKNOWLEDGMENT OF THE PROBLEM

This card signifies your recognition and understanding of your desire to numb out or distract with various habits. It can highlight the aspects you have accepted and those you may still be grappling with.

Card 3
RESOURCES AVAILABLE

This card points to the resources and support systems you have available in your life. These may include friends, family, support groups, or internal strengths that can help you in recovery.

Card 4
ACTION TO TAKE

This card suggests a specific action to take or mindset to embody as you begin your recovery journey. It can provide guidance on what to focus on in your day-to-day life or a starting point if you are struggling with where to begin.

Card 5
OUTCOME OR VISION

This card depicts the broader vision of what sobriety and recovery could look like for you. It can give insight into the potential transformation you may experience.

How to Use This Spread

1. **PREPARE YOUR SPACE**: Find a quiet space where you can reflect. You may wish to light a candle or have some calming music in the background—whatever makes you feel comfortable and at ease with as few interruptions as possible.

2. **CLEAR YOUR MIND**: Take a few deep breaths to center yourself. Focus on your intention for this reading. Know that whatever comes through is never set in stone but merely a guide to provide points to consider and reflect upon.

3. **SHUFFLE AND DRAW YOUR CARDS**: Shuffle your tarot deck while holding your intention in your mind. Once you feel ready, draw five cards and lay them out from left to right.

4. **REFLECT ON EACH CARD**: Take your time to consider the meaning of each card in relation to its position. Think about what the imagery in the card brings up for you and how it makes you feel, and consider consulting an additional tarot book or other resource if you need further insight. Journaling about your thoughts and perceptions can be particularly helpful.

5. **TAKE ACTION**: Consider how you can implement the insights from your reading in your daily life as you embark on your recovery journey. Try to remember that small steps and little shifts add up to create major changes.

A SOBRIETY JAR SPELL

— ◇ —

One of my favorite ways to cast spells is with jars. A jar spell reminds me how easy magic can be: we have the ability to tap into our resources and work with whatever we have at our disposal. Many jar spell ingredients can already be found in our kitchens or even in the flora and fauna of our neighborhood. The jar becomes a place to focus our intention and encapsulate our energy, while also being portable.

I created this spell to focus on what I wished to achieve in sobriety and to act as an enchanted support for my inner strength and resilience. I placed it on my Sobriety Altar (which we will create together in the next chapter), but sometimes we need to bring a physical talisman with us, and this spell can also be easily tossed in a bag, carried along for the ride in a car, or set up on your desk or wherever you could use a magical reminder.

Materials Needed

Paper and something to write with
Mirror
Firesafe container and means to start a fire
Jar with a lid
Pink salt (removes negativity and blockages)
Dried orange peel (joy and happiness)
Dried rose petals (heart-opening, self-love)
Rosemary (protection)
Lavender (calming)
Cinnamon (healing)
Bay leaf marked with Sobriety Sigil (see the next section)
Bay leaf marked with your name
Amethyst (enhances sobriety while releasing heavy emotions and negative energy)
Rose quartz (emotional healing and self-love)
Other crystals if you desire
Green candle (good health, healing, and growth; a white candle is a wonderful substitute, as it has the energy of new beginnings)

The Spell

+ Find a quiet space where you won't be disturbed.
+ Take a few deep breaths to center yourself.
+ Reflect on your intentions for this spell. This could include the desire to embrace recovery and to feel supported in sobriety, but

feel free to phrase this in any way that seems true and authentic
to you.

+ Create a sacred space by clearing the energy of the place you have
  designated for this ritual by burning herbs, ringing a bell, or
  spraying salt water.

+ On the piece of paper, write down your feelings about your
  relationship with substances or whatever has brought you to
  this point. Be honest and open. You might write phrases like *I
  acknowledge my struggles* or *I seek the strength to change* or *I embark
  upon my new journey substance-free*—whatever aligns best for you in
  this moment.

+ If you have a mirror, hold it in front of you and gaze into your
  own eyes. Speak aloud your commitment to yourself: "I accept my
  truth and begin my journey." Allow yourself to feel any emotions
  that arise.

+ Once you've expressed your thoughts, fold the paper and burn it
  (carefully!) in a firesafe dish or cauldron. Visualize the release of
  those burdens as the paper burns. This represents letting go of the
  hold addiction has on you.

+ Take a moment to sit in silence. Visualize yourself embracing
  recovery, feeling lighter and empowered. Repeat a mantra such as
  "I am on the path to healing" or "I accept my journey."

+ Take your small jar and add about a tablespoon of pink salt.
  As you do this, visualize it purifying the space and your intent
  for sobriety.

+ Next, add a tablespoon each of the orange peel, rose, rosemary,
  lavender, and cinnamon. As you add each ingredient to the jar,
  speak or think about your intention, reinforcing your goals and
  desires for sobriety and expressing your gratitude for the energy
  each ingredient brings.

+ Crumble both bay leaves and add them to the jar.
+ Once the ashes from the paper have cooled, add those as well.
+ Add the crystals to the jar. As you add each stone, say a little affirmation or phrase that resonates with your journey. For example, "This crystal brings me strength and clarity" or "This crystal opens my heart."
+ Close the lid of the jar and hold it in your hands with your eyes closed. Hold your intention in your mind as you imagine a white light emanating from your heart, extending from your chest down your arms, through your fingertips, and infusing all the ingredients in the jar with this beautiful energy to support you in your sobriety.
+ Place the jar on your altar and light the green candle. (My preference is a tea light that can be set on top of the lid of the jar, but you can place one next to the jar instead.)
+ When you are ready, conclude the ritual. It's best to never leave a candle burning unattended, so if you must extinguish the candle, snuff it out, rather than blowing it out for this particular spell. Thank any energies or guides you felt present during the ritual.

After the spell, take a moment to journal about the experience. Consider what actions you can take to further your journey in recovery, such as seeking support or educating yourself about sobriety.

Whenever you need a reminder of your strength or a boost of motivation, you may hold the jar or light another candle to place with it and spend some time reflecting through meditation. Let this spell serve as a reminder of your commitment to your sobriety!

CRAFT A SOBRIETY SIGIL

— ◇ —

A sigil is a symbol or pictorial design created to represent a specific intention, desire, or goal magically charged for manifestation.

To begin, clearly articulate what you want to manifest and write it as a simple, positive statement in the present tense as if it has already happened. Since we are speaking specifically about sobriety, you could keep it short, sweet, and to the point with *I am sober*. Or you could expand on it with something like *I feel calm and confident in my sobriety*. My first Sobriety Sigil was based on the intention *I am content in sobriety*. Spend time considering what you truly wish to manifest with your sobriety, how you want to feel, or how you feel you could benefit from more support, and let that be the basis for your intention.

When you have settled on your desire, write it out as a sentence and then remove all of the vowels (*A, E, I, O, U*) from your statement. Next, remove any repeated consonants to simplify the phrase further. For example, with my original intention, I was left with *MCNTSBRY*. Start playing around with the remaining letters—their shapes and forms—to design a graphic representation. You can combine, overlap, rotate, or stylize the letters until you find a design that speaks to you. There are no limits or strict rules here: you cannot make a mistake! Be playful, have fun, and let your creativity and intuition guide you!

Once you have your sigil, concentrate on your intention and visualize your goal or emotional state as you focus on it. Now we are going to charge up the sigil or turn it on energetically. There are various ways to do this including meditating with the sigil and infusing it with your energy and intent, using the sigil in a ritual that aligns with your intention, and visualizing your intention manifesting while looking at the sigil. Whichever you use, know that your intention has been released into the Universe!

To work with your sigil in a ritual, you could carve it into a candle, write it on a piece of paper and rip it up or burn it, draw it on your body with makeup or nontoxic ink (or even just trace it with your fingertips on your skin), or mark it on the soles of your shoes. I drew my sigil on the cover of my tarot journal for my daily card pull reflections, carved it into candles to charge up my Sobriety Jar Spell, and drew it on a piece of paper to keep on my altar. Place your sigil wherever feels right to you and wherever you need a reminder of what you are cocreating with your higher power and the Universe.

THE MAGICIAN AND THE HIGH PRIESTESS

◇ ✧ ◇

BY EMBRACING A BELIEF IN MAGIC,
I KNOW THAT EVERYTHING IS CONNECTED
AND I AM NEVER ALONE.

◇ ✧ ◇

Getting sober is an act of transformation—a great magical working. Now that I had admitted I had a problem, I wanted this attempt at sobriety to be different, so I knew I had to approach it differently. I decided that in addition to going to recovery meetings regularly and my daily tarot practice, I would treat my sobriety like magic.

I created an altar to my sobriety. This is where I would begin and end every day with reflection. At first it was simply where I sat with my tarot cards and my journal, but it quickly became my sanctuary, a place to reconnect with my spiritual practice. In recovery, step two advises that we "believe that a Power greater than ourselves could restore us to sanity." And in the tarot, the two cards that follow the Fool who sets us on the path—the Magician and the High Priestess—show us how to get in touch with our own personal power and higher self: our activation and agency through the Magician and our intuition and inner wisdom through the High Priestess.

THE MAGICIAN

— ◇ —

Manifestation, Creation, Resourcefulness,
Personal Power, Focus, Will, Transformation,
Our Connection to Spirituality

The Magician speaks to harnessing our own skills and resources to effect change, encouraging us to recognize our agency and potential for growth. Associated with manifestation, he's the ultimate creator, showing us that we have the means to turn our visions into reality and bring about meaningful change. In the context of sobriety, this card looks to the power of intention and focused energy in breaking free from addiction.

The Magician knows how to use the tools at his disposal, and for someone in recovery, our tools are therapy, support groups, personal coping strategies, all the resources that help maintain sobriety. Our connection is a power greater than ourselves. This card is also about taking control and mastering your environment rather than being controlled by it. That means reclaiming our personal power, making conscious choices, and committing to a sober lifestyle as a means to restore us to sanity.

At his core, the Magician is about focus and determination. Sobriety requires resolve, a steady commitment to the path ahead. This card can remind you of your own power to overcome obstacles and how, through dedication and skill, you can transform your life and identity beyond addiction.

The Magician is often seen as a bridge between the spiritual and physical realms. In step two of recovery, we cross that bridge. We realize we can tap into something greater than ourselves for our recovery journey. But here's the key: *you* get to define your higher power. It doesn't need to be God in the traditional sense. It can be anything you believe is a source of strength and guidance or a greater force in the Universe, whether that's nature, science, the magic that connects us all, or something else entirely. Your Higher Power should be something that resonates for *you* and provides a sense of meaning and purpose to guide you in your sober journey.

THE HIGH PRIESTESS

— ◇ —

Intuition, Mystery, Sacred Silence, Divine
Feminine, Liminal Space, Stillness

A strong complement to the Magician, the High Priestess represents intuition, inner wisdom, and the mysteries of the subconscious. In sobriety, she calls us to look inward—to understand our triggers, cravings, and emotions. Recovery often requires deep self-reflection, and she shows us the importance of listening to that inner voice, uncovering our hidden truths, and facing the deeper issues that may have fueled addiction.

She also teaches patience and trust in the unknown. Sobriety is rarely a straight path—it's a journey filled with uncertainty. The High Priestess knows healing takes time and can't be rushed. Instead of focusing only on the end goal, she encourages us to embrace the process.

Understanding how past experiences and the unconscious mind shape current behaviors can be key in building a healthier, stabler future. The High Priestess guides us to emotional healing through spiritual wisdom—whether through meditation, therapy, or community support, she encourages seeking deeper insight and connection. In sobriety, this spiritual engagement can provide clarity, strength, and a sense of purpose.

Both cards reinforce that coming to believe in a power greater than oneself is both a passive form of acceptance and an active pursuit. The Magician is the *outer work* (active steps, rebuilding life, setting goals), while the High Priestess is the *inner work* (self-discovery, emotional healing, and spiritual insight). The Magician's drive without the High Priestess's wisdom could lead to burnout or relapse. The High Priestess's introspection without the Magician's action could lead to stagnation. These two archetypes remind us that sobriety isn't just about stopping a behavior—it's about *creating a new life with awareness and purpose.* Embracing both energies can help you navigate the challenges of recovery with both determination and inner peace.

THE TWOS OF THE MINOR ARCANA

Shifting to the Minor Arcana, the Twos represent duality, balance, and decisions. We are now making choices relating to how to utilize this energy of new beginnings and taking the first steps toward manifesting that potential by engaging with another force or perspective.

Let's look at how the energy behind each Two relates to sobriety.

Two of Wands
NEW POSSIBILITIES AND POTENTIAL WITH SOBRIETY

This card speaks to planning, foresight, and the potential for new beginnings. It encourages us to look ahead, set intentions, and explore new paths. I like to think of this card as envisioning a sober future and taking proactive steps toward achieving personal goals. It embodies the optimism and courage needed to embrace change.

Two of Cups
MUTUAL SUPPORT AND PERSONAL
CONNECTIONS IN SOBRIETY

This card tells of partnership, attraction, and the importance of supportive relationships. It can represent the value of a support system, such as friendships or recovery groups that promote healthy connections and emotional healing. It also emphasizes the importance of nurturing positive relationships that foster growth.

Two of Swords
THE INTERNAL STRUGGLE
OF SOBRIETY

The Two of Swords points to difficult choices and the need for inner conflict resolution. It can express the struggle between continuing certain habits and the desire for sobriety. This card highlights the necessity of making clear, conscious decisions and the importance of facing our fears and doubts in the recovery process.

Two of Pentacles
MAINTAINING YOUR EQUILIBRIUM
THROUGH SOBRIETY

This card illustrates the juggling of multiple priorities. In sobriety, it suggests the need to balance various aspects of life, such as work, relationships, and personal time, while still navigating the challenges of recovery. It encourages us to find our own equilibrium, manage stress, and maintain healthy lifestyles without resorting to substances.

⌁⚬⌁

Overall, the Twos announce themes crucial in the journey of sobriety. They encourage self-reflection, accountability, and positive social connections, which can greatly aid in the recovery process. When we are faced with challenges, these cards remind us to seek support, make conscious choices, and work on equilibrium in life. The duality of these cards makes us aware of the other forces we are pairing our energy with—an idea I find quite powerful, because we must be mindful of anything we place in front of or entangle with our sobriety.

GATHERING ITEMS FOR YOUR SOBRIETY ALTAR

— ◇ —

An altar is a dedicated space to center and connect ourselves with our inner wisdom and our higher power. I have numerous altars in my home, each with a different purpose. Early in my sobriety, I built a new one that became my Sobriety Altar, focused on encouraging, supporting, and inspiring my path of recovery. I still spend time at my Sobriety Altar and have expanded its purpose to encompass honoring those who are still suffering in addiction as well as those affected by the suffering of others in addiction and those we have lost due to this turmoil.

There are so many potential benefits of a space dedicated to our sobriety: finding relief from the burden of carrying our problems all on our own, contemplating how circumstances can affect our situation, embracing spiritual growth, understanding the differences between what we can control and what we can't (crucial!), taking a humbler approach to life, becoming more open to making changes in our behavior, and developing a greater sense of personal accountability for the things we do have control over, all while guided by our higher power (more to come on that in the next chapter!).

Creating an altar for sobriety is a meaningful move in our spiritual practice. An altar can serve as a physical reminder of our commitment to sobriety, a space for reflection and meditation, and a focal point for our intentions. Select a quiet and comfortable space in your home where you can set one up. This could be a small table, shelf, or even a windowsill. Just make sure it's a place you can visit regularly.

Here are some ideas for you, based on what I included on my initial Sobriety Altar:

A Tarot Card or Two

I always have the Temperance card on this altar followed by a secondary card to support the aspect of sobriety I am currently working on. This could be the Empress if I need to show myself more kindness, the Queen of Swords if I need to uphold better boundaries, the Ten of Cups if I need to reflect on gratitude, etc. What is it about your sobriety you need support on in this moment?

Crystals

There are so many beautiful crystals with energy supporting sobriety, but amethyst is a wonderful choice for early days. If you are interested in the energetic support of crystals as a helpful talisman, I have included a list of options to enhance your sober intentions (see page 31).

Animal Guide

Animals are so wise, and they offer natural wisdom to us as well. Unicorns became a guiding light for me in early recovery because they are considered a symbol of the divine and often associated with healing, heightened intuition, and the magic of transformation through the journey toward personal truth and inner strength. I felt such inspiration and encouragement from this reminder to seek purity of heart, embrace individuality, and remain open to the magic and mysteries of life through spiritual connection. If there is an animal whose symbolism feels comforting and aligned for you, place some representation of them, such as a photo or figurine, on your altar to serve as energetic encouragement and support.

Sober Inspiration

Not everyone feels comfortable sharing about their sobriety, especially when they're in the public eye, but the world is changing and more people are letting themselves be vulnerable about their mental health and personal journeys. When I was thinking about getting sober, I read an interview with one of my favorite singers, Florence Welch, where she openly spoke about her personal struggles and her sobriety. Watching clips of her concerts, I was struck by how commanding she was in front of an immense crowd of people. Her music was a powerful spell, and she maintained the spotlight with what seemed like unwavering confidence. I thought if she could do that sober, maybe I could do my day-to-day life sober, too. It's wonderful to have examples to admire and inspire!

Who inspires you to stay sober? It doesn't have to be a celebrity; everyone's journey is powerful. Feature a photo or reminder of that person on your altar. What do you wish to accomplish in sobriety? Display pictures of that as well. I wanted to be well enough to build and maintain a successful business with my witchcraft, so on my altar, I placed a dollar alongside photos of Laurie Cabot (the official witch of Salem, the first professional witch I had ever encountered), Miss Cleo (the TV psychic from my childhood), and Glinda the Good Witch from *The Wizard of Oz*. Even though I self-identified as a magical lone wolf, I longed to be part of a community of witches, so I also put up a postcard with a vintage photo called "Circle of Witches Dancing," which depicted a group of women holding hands beneath a weeping willow in the throes of an enchanted trance. I hoped that could be my future in sobriety with a coven I didn't know yet.

I encourage you to consider some of the hobbies and interests that used to bring you joy and employ your altar as a way to reestablish or deepen your connection with them. This could inspire you to dedicate more time to these endeavors without substances. It's also inspiring to include personal items that represent your journey so far, such as coins or stones you've collected or photographs of special memories. One of my dear friends had a medallion made for me in celebration of my first year of sobriety, and I still keep it on my altar.

Candles

Light symbolizes hope and renewal. You might choose a candle for each area of your life that your sobriety impacts. (See my suggestions for colors on page 35.) I have a candleholder that I drew my Sobriety Sigil on. You could do the same or carve it into your candles.

Personal Symbols and Things You Love

My reliance on substances made me lose touch with so many interests I loved, and getting sober offered an opportunity to reconnect with those aspects of my life. I love being by the ocean, so I included seashells on my altar. I have always loved art, and at this time in my life, I was working in the art world and trying to figure out my place and my path, so I included an image of my favorite Hilma af Klint painting because of how she applied her spirituality and mediumship in her work. I also included a small book of love poems because poetry was something I always enjoyed as a teenager but hadn't made much time for as an adult.

Write or print quotes that motivate and inspire you. You can also incorporate art or music that uplifts your spirit.

Plants

Nature elements can add life and positive energy to your altar. For some flowers for sobriety, see page 33.

Journals or Notebooks

Give yourself a space to write your thoughts, intentions, or affirmations when you are at your altar. Periodically spend some time reflecting on what sobriety means to you. Consider putting down your intentions, goals, and affirmations related to your sobriety and placing these somewhere on or near the altar.

BUILDING YOUR SOBRIETY ALTAR

— ◇ —

There are no strict rules, but here are some suggestions for how to arrange your altar.

Choose a central focus, like a candle or a statue, that represents your commitment to sobriety. Place your other items around the centerpiece in a way that feels balanced and harmonious. Use varying heights and textures to create visual interest. This is a very special place for you, so treat it as such! Make it feel inviting, exciting, and inspiring to be with your altar. This is an act of devotion!

Make the altar uniquely yours. Over time, add new items or change things up as your journey evolves. This can keep the space fresh and resonant with your current state of being.

Visit your altar regularly: daily, weekly, or whenever you feel the need for support. Use it as a place for contemplation, motivation, and connection to your higher self or spiritual beliefs. Light candles as a daily or weekly practice to signal your commitment.

Spend a few moments in mindful silence and meditation, focusing on your breath or the intention behind your sobriety. Journal about your journey, reflecting on your progress or expressing gratitude. Consider using your altar to mark significant dates in your sobriety journey, such as anniversaries or milestones. You can add small tokens or notes to commemorate these moments.

Stay open to change and allow your altar to evolve as you do. If you find that certain items no longer serve you, feel free to remove them or replace them with new symbols of your journey. *Trust your intuition.* Ultimately, your Sobriety Altar is a personal representation of your journey. Rely on your instincts when selecting items and creating a space that feels right for you. Building an altar for your sobriety is a deeply personal experience, helping to cultivate a sense of peace, reflection, and commitment to your path. Embrace the process and let it be a source of strength, inspiration, and deeper connection.

CRYSTALS FOR SOBRIETY

— ◇ —

Many people believe that certain crystals can help support sobriety and recovery by promoting emotional healing, mental clarity, and inner strength. Here are some of my favorites commonly associated with these intentions:

AMETHYST: Known for its calming properties, amethyst is believed to help with addiction by providing clarity and aiding in decision-making. It promotes emotional balance and helps alleviate stress.

BLACK TOURMALINE: This stone is believed to offer protection from negative energies and promote emotional stability. It's often used to ground individuals and provide a sense of security during challenging times.

CARNELIAN: This stone is believed to boost motivation and courage. Its energizing properties can help people in recovery take inspired action toward our goals.

CITRINE: This crystal is linked to positivity and motivation. Citrine is believed to encourage inner strength and personal will, which can be beneficial for maintaining sobriety.

CLEAR QUARTZ: Often referred to as the "master healer," clear quartz is thought to amplify positive energy and thoughts. It's also said to help with focus and clarity, making it a great choice for recovery work.

LAPIS LAZULI: This stone is thought to encourage self-awareness and self-expression. It can assist in facing our emotions and can be a supportive companion during difficult times.

MOONSTONE: Associated with intuition and emotional balance, moonstone can help us stay in touch with our feelings, which can be important in the recovery process.

ROSE QUARTZ: Often called the stone of love, rose quartz promotes self-love and compassion. It can aid in emotional healing and self-acceptance, which are crucial in recovery.

SODALITE: Known for shoring up self-esteem and self-acceptance, sodalite can help us confront our emotions and promote inner peace, making it beneficial during recovery.

TIGEREYE: Known for grounding and protective qualities, tigereye can help with confidence and overcoming fear, providing support during the ups and downs of recovery.

While crystals can serve as supportive tools, it is important to remember that recovery is a complex process that often requires professional guidance as well as personal commitment. Integrating crystals into a recovery journey can be complementary to a broader support system. It's wonderful to create a multidimensional approach of what works for you and resonates to remind you of your inherent strength and agency, while keeping in mind one of my favorite recovery adages: take what you need and leave the rest!

FLOWERS FOR SOBRIETY

— ◇ —

In addition to their symbolic meanings, incorporating flowers into a recovery space can enhance the environment by making it more beautiful, comforting, and serene. It's essential to remember that personal connections to flowers can vary, so individuals may find their own favorites that feel right for their journeys. Be open to the exploration of what works for you!

Create a bouquet for your Sobriety Altar or another place within your home to remind you of the assistance available to you. Allow the frequencies of the flowers to shift and change to bolster your intentions as needed. In my early recovery, I wanted reminders of joy, self-love, and compassion and chose flowers that evoked those things. It was such a lovely experience to have them brighten my bedroom! I also used an assortment of these flowers in ritual baths as well.

Here are some flowers often associated with positive energy, healing, and emotional support:

CHAMOMILE: Often used in teas, chamomile has soothing effects that can help with stress and promote restful sleep. I love sprinkling them into a bath for a bedtime meditation ritual.

DAISY: Representing innocence and new beginnings, daisies can remind us of the beauty of starting fresh and embracing a new path.

GERBERA DAISY: Known for their vibrant colors, Gerbera daisies signify cheerfulness and positivity, which can be uplifting during the recovery process. These provide an instant boost of happiness!

HIBISCUS: Known for its bright colors and tropical feel, hibiscus symbolizes beauty and joy, fostering a positive atmosphere.

JASMINE: This flower is often associated with love and beauty. Its sweet fragrance can have uplifting effects and promote a sense of well-being.

LAVENDER: Known for its calming properties, lavender can reduce anxiety and promote relaxation.

LOTUS: In many cultures, the lotus flower symbolizes rebirth and purity, which can resonate deeply with those of us in recovery as we seek to rise above past struggles.

PEONY: Often associated with healing and compassion, peonies can bring a sense of hope and renewal.

ROSE: Roses embody love in all its forms, including self-love. Their energy helps us open our hearts to receive love, compassion, and kindness. Different colors of roses can represent various emotions. Pink roses symbolize love and compassion, while white roses signify purity and new beginnings—important themes in recovery.

SUNFLOWER: Symbolizing positivity and warmth, sunflowers can inspire joy and resilience, reminding us of our strength and ability to overcome challenges.

COLOR MAGIC FOR SOBRIETY SUPPORT

— ◇ —

Colors carry specific energetic properties that can influence mood, behavior, and overall well-being. By incorporating color magic into everyday life, we can create a more supportive environment that promotes healing and positive change. By consciously using colors in daily life, we can harness their energetic properties to aid in the journey of sobriety and recovery. Remember that color associations can be personal; what works for one person may not resonate with another, so it's important to find what feels right for you.

Some easy ways to utilize the healing and empowering frequency of color include wearing clothing in colors that meet your current needs and emotional state; decorating your home with paint, fabrics, or accessories in specific colors to create an environment that fosters healing; incorporating colors into meditation or visualization exercises, focusing on their properties and how they influence your recovery; bringing these colors into your Sobriety Altar with candles, crystals, and other talismans in a shade that offers the energetic support you need or enhances your recovery intentions; and engaging in creative activities using different colors for expressing and exploring your emotions.

RED: Confidence, strength, passion. Can empower us by instilling confidence and determination but should be used mindfully to avoid triggering intensity or aggressive feelings.

PINK: Love, compassion, nurturing. Promotes self-love and compassion, which are vital in the recovery journey.

ORANGE: Creativity, enthusiasm, success. Stimulates, motivates, and provides inspiration and a sense of adventure.

YELLOW: Joy, optimism, clarity. Uplifts mood, enhances self-esteem, and promotes a positive outlook.

GREEN: Healing, growth, abundance, balance. Symbolizes renewal and the healing process, fostering a sense of balance and stability.

BLUE: Calm, peace, openness. Aids in communication and self-expression and helps reduce anxiety.

PURPLE: Spiritual growth, intuition, transformation. Encourages deep self-reflection and spiritual healing.

WHITE: Cleansing, clarity, new beginnings. Represents a fresh start and a blank slate, ideal for setting new intentions.

BROWN: Groundedness, stability, healing. Provides a sense of stability and safety, helping to feel rooted during times of uncertainty.

BLACK: Boundaries, protection, resolve. Absorbs and repels negative influences while providing protection and strengthening energetic boundaries.

A TAROT SPREAD FOR STEP TWO: INTEGRATING YOUR HIGHER POWER

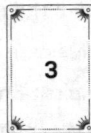

— ◇ —

```
┌─────────┐
│    1    │
└─────────┘

┌─────────┐
│    2    │
└─────────┘

┌─────────┐
│    3    │
└─────────┘
```

This tarot spread corresponds to understanding, embodying, and integrating the concept of a higher power in your practice.

Card 1

UNDERSTANDING MY HIGHER POWER

What does this card say about your understanding of a higher power? Consider how it resonates with your personal beliefs or experiences.

This card represents your current perception of a higher power. It will give insight into what "greater than myself" means to you at this moment.

Card 2

HOW TO EMBODY
FAITH AND ACCEPTANCE

How does this card suggest you can embody the faith required in this step? Look for the practical actions or mental shifts it inspires.

This card will help you explore ways to actively embody the belief in this higher power and the acceptance of support. It may suggest acts or attitudes that can help you cultivate faith.

Card 3

INTEGRATION OF THIS
BELIEF IN MY DAILY LIFE

What guidance does this card offer for embodying this belief in your life? Think about how you can make this a consistent part of your recovery journey.

This card illustrates how you can integrate this belief into your routine and daily recovery process. It may provide guidance on how to align your actions with this newfound understanding.

As you shuffle the cards, focus on the intention of seeking clarity on step two of your recovery. Draw three cards and place them in front of you in a line. Reflect on each card guided by the prompts provided. Write down impressions and insights from each card, noting any feelings or ideas that arise. Consider how these reflect your current experience with recovery and your relationship with a higher power. From these reflections, identify one or two concrete steps you can take to embody the guidance from your reading in your daily life.

A STEP TWO RITUAL:
INVITING IN A POWER
GREATER THAN OURSELVES

— ◇ —

Step two in recovery asks us to believe that "a Power greater than ourselves can restore us to sanity." For many of us, this step can feel abstract or even uncomfortable—especially if our past experiences with spirituality were painful, dogmatic, or absent altogether. This ritual creates space to approach that idea gently, on your own terms, through the language of intention, symbolism, and sacred connection.

This is not about getting the "right" answers—it's about creating a channel for spiritual connection that feels true to you. Whether you call it God, Goddess, the Universe, Spirit, Love, or simply something greater, this ritual allows you to invite that energy in with intention and openness.

Materials Needed

Small table or flat surface for your altar
White or light blue cloth (representing purity and healing)
Candle (white for clarity or light blue for tranquility) and a means to light it

Small bowl of water (symbolizing emotional healing)
Piece of paper and pen
Fresh flowers or herbs that resonate with you (optional)

The Spell

+ Set up your altar with the cloth, placing the candle in the center. Put the bowl of water next to the candle.

+ Cleanse your space by lighting some incense or use a cleansing herb (like lavender or rosemary) to purify the space. As you do this, say: "I cleanse this space of all negativity. Only positive energy surrounds me."

+ Set your intention by sitting before your altar and taking a few deep breaths. Think about how you would like to invite a greater power into your life. Use the paper to write down your intentions or a letter to your higher power. You might express your need for guidance, strength, and healing in your recovery journey.

+ Light the candle and say: "With this flame, I call in light, a guiding force to show me right. In my heart, I make this vow to trust in you, I ask for now."

+ Dip your fingers in the bowl of water. As you do, visualize the water as a source of healing, washing away doubt and fear. Say out loud: "As water flows and cleanses me, I open my heart to what I can't see. I trust the journey, step-by-step. With each drop, my burdens are swept."

+ Spend a few moments in quiet meditation. Focus on your breath and visualize your greater power surrounding you with love and protection.

+ After your meditation, thank your higher power and any spiritual guides you feel connected to.

+ Snuff out the candle to signify the end of your ritual. Place your intention letter under the candle or in the bowl of water as a reminder of your commitment to sobriety.

This spell is not just a onetime event but a continuous practice. Return to your Sobriety Altar whenever you need to reaffirm your commitment to sobriety, and use it as a tool for reflection and empowerment. Remember: your journey is unique, and honoring it through ritual can deepen your connection to your recovery path.

THE EMPRESS AND THE EMPEROR

❖ ❖ ❖

BY NURTURING MYSELF, I MAKE
EMPOWERED DECISIONS.

❖ ❖ ❖

Every step of the way in early sobriety, our brains will try to trick us into holding on to our addictions and our precious demons by abandoning this new path. One of the most beautiful things I have learned in sobriety is how deeply rewarding it is to do things that feel scary, allow myself to be uncomfortable, and get through it to the other side.

Step three of recovery says we "Made a decision to turn our will and our lives over to the care of a higher power as we understood it." This is one of those uncomfortable moments I see people using as an excuse to leave the process behind—when *God* enters the chat through the notion of a higher power. It's where I've had problems myself in the past. More traditional monotheistic twelve-step programs can feel cold and exclusionary when you're coming from a pagan or other nature-based spiritual belief system.

The reality is that sobriety is not easy and can be uncomfortable, but any major change, any first steps in healing that take you on the path toward greatness are going to be difficult. These difficulties never last forever; nothing does. So along the way, it's worth finding support and comfort in the unknown by calling upon your higher power—whatever that might look like for you.

Your higher power can be anything: the Universe, nature, a specific spirit. It just needs to remind you there is something beyond yourself in this moment. This is your opportunity to give yourself over to your highest good in the search to do better and to be better. This is an opportunity to trust and understand that recovery is not a journey you need to embark on on your own. We are all the masters of our own destiny, but faith helps us achieve the seemingly impossible. There is far less pressure when you understand you can be guided through this journey of recovery by a power greater than yourself.

To do something as powerful as fully committing to sobriety, I knew I needed the support of a powerful deity—someone who wasn't only unafraid of the dark but thrived in it unapologetically and was fluent in the language of the shadows. I called upon someone I used to know quite well but hadn't been ready to commit to in the past. I called upon Lilith.

In college, I lived blocks from the Museum of Fine Arts in Boston and would make many hungover and high pilgrimages there to my version of church on Sunday mornings: wandering its halls and trying to get out of my own head. Near the entrance, I remember locking eyes with the haunting sculpture of a nude woman with glass eyes crouched upside down and perpendicular to a white wall overhead. Her gaze seared through me, and I would look down to avoid making eye contact—like I would avoid eye contact with my mom when I would come home high as a kite or drunk out of my mind as a teenager. This figure had that same all-knowing energy of my mom, as if she could somehow see what I had been up to the night before and did not approve. I scooted right by her and into the farthest corners of the museum where she couldn't judge me.

After weeks of this, I finally went over to read the tag on the wall to see who this could be. "*Lilith* by Kiki Smith." *Oh, I know you,* I thought, *the infamous scorned woman, the first wife of Adam who was cast out of Eden for being too brazen, too bold, too lusty, too much herself, who refused to be submissive to her partner and demanded to be treated as an equal.* I liked her whole vibe: unapologetically powerful, the complete opposite of how I felt but how I aspired to be. And even though her energy felt unattainable, there was something in her that reminded me of the ultimate demonic party girl—so cool she probably didn't need any substances to remind her of her own power.

At the same time, I was taking Metaphysical Kung Fu classes with Peter Valentine, an outsider artist in Cambridge who was helping me understand my psychic powers by harnessing my energy field and learning how to manipulate energy with my mind. After class, I would sit with Peter and ask him all my existential questions, and his simplest answers always made the most sense. He once told me, "We inherently know what we need and are drawn to it." His wise words echoed in my mind as I was pulled to Lilith.

I felt compelled to talk to her and share my immense emotions and never-ending problems, but there was just no way I could endlessly chat with her in such a public place as the entrance of the MFA, so I began to go to a far corner of the museum grounds and sit by a thorny bramble of a bush. I figured if it felt like she could see what I had been up to when I was out at night, she could hear me in such close proximity to her sculpture, too. I closed my eyes and tried to think of what to do next.

I remembered my first witchcraft book, *To Ride a Silver Broomstick* by Silver RavenWolf, which had become my bible when I was twelve, had taught me the importance of making offerings to your goddesses. Everyone loves gifts, including deities, and our presents show our deep devotion and gratitude for their presence and guidance in our lives. I looked through my purse perennially overflowing with junk and considered what was valuable to me, what would be a little bit painful to do without, and what a demonic party girl might like. I threw down my favorite lipstick and a cigarette from my yellow pack of American Spirits. And then I added another—anyone I encountered on the street could bum a cigarette from me, but offering two felt like a real gift because it pained me a bit more. I unclipped one of my ratty black hair extensions and threw that in, too. What I have learned from magic is to trust my intuition: if something feels right, you should do it, even if doesn't make sense just yet.

This became my ritual. Once a week, I would drag my hungover body out of bed, eyes smeared with days and nights of old makeup, head pounding, fighting off nausea, and go to this far corner outside of the museum to talk to Lilith. I would pour mini bottles of blush Sutter Home wine into the soil and scatter red rose petals for her. I would tell her what was going on and try to cry. It was very difficult to feel anything other than a murky cloud of dull despair, but I gave it my all for her. Was this truly an act of devotion or just juvenile complaining? Maybe it was both.

I don't remember when I stopped visiting Lilith, but I maintained a relationship with her that shape-shifted throughout the years. That's the incredible part of deity worship: they always let you know they are around even if your devotion waxes and wanes. When you remain open to the signs, you will spot them in abundance. And when I recommitted to sobriety, I recommitted to my relationship with Lilith.

I had been noticing the signs of her everywhere as she offered reminders that she was still with me: intense dreams of black snakes that felt protective rather than frightening; a song about Lilith that came on when I started my car; pomegranates, the fruit of forbidden knowledge, on deep discount at the grocery store; my old Lilith Fair poster rediscovered in my parents' home; a book of mythology featuring Lilith on the cover I literally tripped over in the used bookstore. (I know! Even I could barely believe that last one!)

Were these coincidences? Maybe, but I don't believe in those, and the signs were becoming quite difficult to ignore. And why should I? I was asking for help—and here it was. So for the very first time in a very long time, I built her an altar on a small shelf in my room. Everything else was lost, all the physical identifiers of who I thought I was, and I was ready to surrender to the assistance and support being offered by such a powerful guide.

Step three in twelve-step programs is about relinquishing control. There is an epic amount of supposed control and management involved in the upkeep of an addiction. ("I am allowed to have three drinks tonight." Or, "I can drink wine but not liquor." All the made-up rules we impose on ourselves to create the illusion that we are in charge of the addiction and not the other way around.) True surrender brings freedom, and reconnecting with a powerful deity like Lilith to guide me through that first year brought me back to the freedom of true power and agency—something I'd lost along the way.

Lilith is a powerful archetype of feminine independence, rebellion, and self-determination. Sobriety is a radical act of rebellion, and she is a lovely guide to remind us of how inherently incredible an act this can be! Lilith allows individuals to explore and embrace their own shadow aspects, particularly when seeking to break free from societal expectations and claim personal power in their lives. She embodies a fierce, untamed energy that can be empowering for those seeking to reclaim their autonomy—and as we know, sobriety is also a reclamation of one's own power!

Lilith is a notoriously challenging energy to work with, but so is an addict: it's not like getting sober is easy. I love a challenge, and she is fiercely protective and loyal to those she deems worthy. I celebrated my first year of sobriety by getting a tattoo of her symbol on my inner wrist, where it is immediately and prominently visible when I shuffle my tarot cards. After all these years, she is still guiding me, and she's always with me through any reading.

As we follow the Fool's Journey through the Major Arcana, we are next greeted by the Empress and the Emperor, or as I like to call them, the parents of the tarot family. The Empress is a nurturing maternal figure who guides through her love and support, while the Emperor provides structure and discipline.

THE EMPRESS

— ◇ —

Nurturing, Abundance, Creativity,
Compassion, Connection to Nature

With a warm and caring presence, the Empress expresses the importance of self-care and nurturing oneself during the healing process of sobriety. Recovery requires individuals to cultivate self-love and compassion, a bottom-up agency that aligns with the Empress's energy of fertility. Recovery can be considered a rebirth, giving individuals the opportunity to create a new life built on health and well-being. The Empress is all about embracing creativity and finding joy in new experiences. The Empress is also often associated with nature and the earth, and reconnecting with nature can be a powerful healing force for those of us in recovery, promoting mindfulness and tranquility.

THE EMPEROR

— ◇ —

Structure, Stability, Discipline,
Control, Supportive Authority

The Emperor speaks to us of authority, structure, and stability. In the context of recovery, this card is about establishing solid foundations and routines that support a sober lifestyle. Having a structured approach can be crucial for making thoughtful decisions and maintaining sobriety. The Emperor's discipline and assertiveness are qualities that can be essential for individuals navigating the challenges of addiction recovery. This card encourages taking responsibility for our actions and setting the boundaries that protect our sobriety. The Emperor can also suggest the presence of a mentor or supportive figure in our recovery journey. This could be a counselor, sponsor, or family member who helps provide guidance and accountability.

⌒──☀──⌒

Considered together, these cards highlight a harmonious balance between nurturing oneself (Empress) and establishing structure (Emperor). A successful recovery journey often requires both kindness to oneself and the discipline to maintain healthy boundaries and consistent routines. In essence, the relationship between the Empress and the Emperor encourages you to foster self-love and creativity while also building a strong framework of discipline and support to navigate your healing journey effectively. It also emphasizes the importance of community and support systems: the nurturing aspect of the Empress can signify the support of friends and family, while the Emperor can represent the structure provided by support groups and recovery programs.

In the context of step three of recovery of making the decision to turn our will and our lives over to the care of a higher power as we understand it, the Emperor and the Empress reflect the balance of surrendering one's will—and all the micromanaging tricks we play on ourselves in addiction—while still cultivating self-care and personal responsibility, all of which are essential for a successful journey toward change and rejuvenation. In the context of step three, surrendering one's will can paradoxically require a sense of inner strength and structure. Surrender isn't about collapse or passivity. It's an intentional act, one that actually calls for a surprising amount of resolve and acceptance of structure. In addiction, our lives were often ruled by chaos, compulsions, and survival patterns. Even if there appeared to be routines or regimens, they were often rigid, fear-based, or reactionary, leaving no room for gentleness, flexibility, or trust.

Surrendering in recovery is different. It's not about giving up in defeat: it's about opening up with purpose. And *that* takes courage, boundaries, and a certain kind of inner scaffolding. Surrender asks us to pause, to listen, to stop trying to control every outcome. That kind of spaciousness can only be held when we've built some daily practices, rituals, tools for regulation, and trusted support systems around ourselves. That structure supports softness, rather than suppressing it.

Surrendering your will is an immense act that allows nurturing, grace, and divine guidance to flow in. And what it needs in order to happen is not the rigidity of addiction but the sacred rhythm of recovery.

THE THREES OF THE MINOR ARCANA

— ✦ —

The Threes of the Minor Arcana offer a holistic approach to recovery, promoting both emotional resilience and the value of relationships as we embark on a new, sober path.

Three of Wands
FUTURE VISION, PLANNING, AND HOPE FOR WHAT'S NEXT

This card symbolizes foresight, expansion, and looking toward the future.

The Three of Wands encourages individuals in recovery to think about their long-term goals and the possibilities that lie ahead. It speaks to their vision of a better future and the importance of planning and preparing for what's next. This means setting intentions for ongoing growth and looking forward to the new opportunities that arise from staying sober.

Three of Cups
COMMUNITY SUPPORT THROUGH SOCIAL CONNECTIONS

The Three of Cups is often associated with celebration, friendship, and community.

Connecting with others, sharing experiences, and celebrating milestones (such as sobriety anniversaries) can be vital for emotional support. It signifies joy found in camaraderie, which is essential for those of us on the path to recovery.

Three of Swords
EMOTIONAL HEALING BY RECOGNIZING AND PROCESSING PAIN AS PART OF THE RECOVERY JOURNEY

The Three of Swords shows us heartbreak, sorrow, and emotional pain.

The Three of Swords acknowledges that the journey of recovery is not without its challenges and emotional struggles. It may represent past traumas or the pain associated with addiction, but it can also point to the necessary confrontation of these difficult emotions in the process of healing. Recognizing and working through this pain is essential for long-term growth.

Three of Pentacles
COLLABORATIVE EFFORTS HIGHLIGHTING TEAMWORK WITH PROFESSIONALS AND PEERS

This card represents teamwork, collaboration, and the mastery of skills.

For recovery, the Three of Pentacles highlights the significance of working with professionals like counselors or therapists, support groups, or peers who are also in recovery. It suggests this is often a collaborative process, where learning from one another and building relationships based on shared goals can facilitate personal growth and stability.

HOW TO FIND AND CONNECT WITH YOUR OWN HIGHER POWER

— ◇ —

Connecting with your higher power, goddess, or deity is a deeply personal and meaningful aspect of a sobriety journey. Here are some practices that helped me you might consider incorporating into your own process.

First, let's define what your higher power means to you: It could be a goddess or deity, the Universe, nature, spirituality, or a concept like love or truth that resonates with you. It's your *personal understanding* of a higher power so it should align with your beliefs. If you are drawn to a particular goddess, learn about her attributes and teachings to understand how they might inspire your journey. Let your research be an adventure. Approach this with an open mind and wonder! Notice what you feel drawn to and let that lead the way as you pair it with any signs you have been noticing in your day-to-day as well as your dreams.

Once you settle upon your definition of a higher power or identify who it could be, create a clear intention by acknowledging what you hope to achieve through your connection with this higher power—such as strength, guidance, healing, and overall support on your sobriety journey. Be open to the idea that your understanding may evolve over time.

Part of beginning your relationship with your higher power is designating a sacred space to commune together. Create a physical place that feels special to you and invites calmness and reflection. This can be an addition to the Sobriety Altar we created in the last chapter or a newly designated spot. Space may be limited if, for example, you have a small apartment or live with roommates, so I love the idea of expanding the Sobriety Altar to include your meeting place with your higher power. That's what I did in my early recovery.

Wherever you choose, this space can include candles, crystals, images of your chosen goddess, or items that hold personal significance to you to offer additional support. Now, this is a very important part: spend time in this space! Set aside time each day for reflection or meditation. This could involve quiet contemplation, journaling, or simply sitting in silence. No matter what your day may entail, make it a goal to begin and end at your altar with your higher power.

Praying can be a way of connecting, whether it's formal or informal. Meditation can also help you listen and be present, opening a pathway to understanding or feeling your higher power. It doesn't need to be a lot, but this sacred time is a gift to you and your sobriety, so dedicate it to focus on your breath, your goals, or the qualities of your higher power. Visualize a connection or guidance flowing toward you. If you need additional support, you can find guided meditations specifically geared toward connecting with deities, spiritual figures, or your inner strength.

Incorporate rituals that honor your goddess or higher power, such as lighting a candle or reciting prayers or affirmations. Consider making offerings that are meaningful to you or that symbolize your journey, like writing your struggles down and releasing them into water or safely burning them. Research what sort of gifts your deity appreciates. You may learn that some enjoy offerings of wine or liquor, but I believe that our higher power always has our best interests in mind, and alcohol on a Sobriety Altar or in a space dedicated to their guidance in our journey feels wildly inappropriate and unnecessarily triggering—instead, I offer a goblet of water among the gifts to my goddess.

Another way to show dedication is through creating affirmations aligned with the qualities of your goddess or higher power. Repeat these daily to reinforce your commitment to sobriety. You could also develop a personal mantra related to your journey like "I am worthy of recovery, wellness, and joy" or "I am not alone in my sobriety" or "I am healing." Choose something that helps you feel how powerful you truly are in your sobriety. Be open to intuitive thoughts, dreams, or signs that may come as guidance from your higher power. I always say that if it *feels* like a sign or a message, then there's no need to question it! Trust your own process and have faith that your connection will strengthen over time.

Document your journey! Write about your experiences, thoughts, and emotions in a journal. This can help you process feelings and track your spiritual growth. Regularly write down what you are grateful for, including the support you receive from your higher power. Practicing this can help you recognize the positive forces in your life and acknowledge the role of your higher power in these moments.

You can also connect with your higher power outside of this dedicated space. Engage in acts of service or kindness toward others as a way to express your gratitude and tap into a larger sense of purpose. Explore books or texts that align with your understanding of a higher power, such as spiritual literature, poetry, or writings from recognized figures in recovery or spirituality.

Incorporating nature into your practice can also be a powerful way to access the divine, grounding yourself and finding clarity through the beauty and serenity of the natural world. Practice being present in the moment and observing the world around you. Pay attention to synchronicities or intuitions that may indicate guidance or support from your higher power.

Develop personal rituals that feel meaningful, such as lighting a candle, creating an altar, or dedicating a specific time each week for spiritual activities. Participate in or create ceremonies that mark important milestones in your sobriety journey.

Your journey is unique, and there's no right or wrong way to connect with a higher power or goddess. Trust your instincts and allow your spirituality to evolve as you grow in your sobriety. Most importantly, maintain a commitment to your practices and beliefs, even during difficult times. Consistency can deepen your connection and understanding. And know that your relationship with a higher power can change and that's OK. Stay flexible and open to new experiences. Remember that everyone's journey in sobriety is unique, and what works for one person may not work for another. Be patient and compassionate with yourself as you explore and nurture your connection with a higher power.

GODDESSES FOR SOBRIETY

— ◇ —

Notable goddesses that make me think of a sobriety journey include ones who can empower us as we explore the shadows. They are fierce and hold great power as they guide us through the darker times in life toward the light. I encourage you to find a guide who connects with your ancestry and resonates with the healing aspects you wish to focus on through your sobriety.

ACESO: Greek goddess of curing sickness and healing wounds, she offers guidance through the process of healing.

ELEOS: Greek goddess of mercy and compassion, Eleos emphasizes understanding rather than judgment, encouraging us to treat ourselves with kindness as we navigate the challenges of sobriety.

HECATE: Goddess of the crossroads, witchcraft, and the moon. Her journey through the Underworld to the Upperworld is reminiscent of the road to recovery, so she is well prepared to guide us through transitions and transformations. Her presence can provide the reassurance that we are not alone, even in dark times.

HEL: Hel, the goddess of the underworld in Norse mythology, embodies the duality of life and death, light and darkness. She serves as a powerful escort through shadow work, encouraging us to confront fears and inner struggles rather than avoid them.

KALI: Kali is a fierce and powerful Hindu goddess who represents strength, empowerment, and independence. Invoking Kali as a guide through sobriety can be an affirmation of our own strength and capacity to overcome obstacles. Often associated with destruction and creation, Kali symbolizes the transformative process of letting go of old habits and embracing a new life.

KUAN YIN: The Bodhisattva of Compassion in Buddhism, Kuan Yin offers support during difficult times and healing energy with the reminder that all deserve unconditional compassion and love. She does not judge and instead provides solace so those of us who are suffering can feel safe in our vulnerability and confront inner challenges without shame.

LILITH: A deity of shadow work who provides courage, authenticity, authority, self-acceptance, and empowerment, Lilith's rebellious nature in rejecting societal norms and expectations is inspiring for sobriety's spurning of societal pressures that may have encouraged alcohol use. Engaging with our shadow leads to deeper self-understanding and processing of past traumas to facilitate healing.

MEDUSA: Goddess of transformation and protection who guides through times of adversity, Medusa embodies strength and resilience despite her tragic fate. She offers the guidance to embrace fears rather than succumbing to them as part of sobriety. Medusa is often misunderstood and vilified in a way that is similar to the stigma surrounding addiction and recovery. By identifying with a misunderstood figure, those of us in sobriety can feel empowered to break the stigma associated with our own struggles.

THE MORRIGAN: The Morrigan is an Irish goddess of profound change, transformation, and empowerment who can offer guidance through significant life transitions such as sobriety.

PERSEPHONE: Persephone's descent into the Underworld can symbolize the confronting of inner demons and struggles through sobriety. Her ascent back to the surface represents personal resilience and the ability to grow from challenging experiences, showing us that renewal and growth are always possible.

SEKHMET: Sekhmet is an Egyptian goddess of healing whose wisdom encompasses strength and resilience, qualities essential for those leading a newly sober lifestyle. Her fierceness can inspire us to confront our struggles with courage and determination while establishing a healthier lifestyle.

SOBRIETAS: This is the Roman equivalent of Sophrosyne, whose name provides the origin of the word *sobriety*. Is there a better spirit to commune with than the namesake herself?

SOPHROSYNE: A benevolent spirit who escaped Pandora's box, she personifies temperance, moderation, self-control, and restraint. Sophrosyne is recognized as a virtue of self-control and moderation to aspire to in one's life.

VENUS: Goddess of self-love, self-care, and beauty, Venus emphasizes emotional well-being and healing to help us work through underlying emotional pain with compassion. She also embodies pleasure and creativity—two aspects of life that are important to reconnect with in healthy ways through sobriety.

A TAROT SPREAD
TO CONNECT WITH YOUR
HIGHER POWER

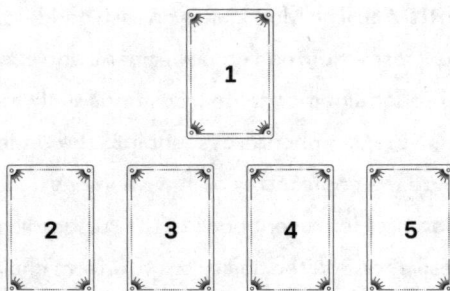

— ◇ —

This tarot spread is designed to help you get better acquainted with your higher power so you can work together on your sobriety journey.

Card 1: A card to represent my higher power

Card 2: A message my higher power wants me to know

Card 3: Something I can do to deepen our connection

Card 4: An aspect of my sobriety I can focus on with my higher power

Card 5: Something I can release in order to facilitate this work

A TRUST
AND SURRENDER
TAROT SPREAD

— ◇ —

```
        ┌─────┐
        │  1  │
        └─────┘

  ┌─────┐   ┌─────┐
  │  2  │   │  3  │
  └─────┘   └─────┘

  ┌─────┐   ┌─────┐
  │  4  │   │  5  │
  └─────┘   └─────┘

        ┌─────┐
        │  6  │
        └─────┘
```

Step three involves making a decision to turn our will and life over to the care of a higher power as we understand it. This step can be both empowering and challenging, as it requires trust, surrender, and open-mindedness. This spread can be a useful tool to explore our feelings about this step, uncover subconscious obstacles, and gain clarity on our path forward.

Card 1
GETTING CURRENT

Represents where you are now in your recovery journey.

Card 2
WHAT TO SURRENDER
AND LET GO OF

Insights into thoughts, behaviors, or situations you need to release to move forward. It might highlight fears, control issues, or old patterns that are holding you back.

Card 3
HIGHER POWER'S GUIDANCE

This card reflects what your higher power wants from you at this point in your recovery. It could be a message of guidance or support or an invitation to deepen your understanding and relationship with your higher power.

Card 4
TRUST AND SURRENDER

What you must embrace to truly surrender and trust the process.

Card 5
NEXT STEPS

Actions or attitudes to embody as you continue on your path.

Card 6
POTENTIAL OUTCOME

This card will provide insight into the benefits and rewards of surrendering control and trusting in a higher power. It may highlight personal growth, peace of mind, or a renewed sense of purpose.

After pulling the cards, spend some time journaling about your insights, feelings, and any actions that might arise from this exploration. Take time to envision the possibilities of how turning over control could impact various areas of your life—relationships, emotional well-being, spirituality, and overall happiness.

A STEP THREE RITUAL TO CONNECT WITH YOUR DEITY

— ◇ —

This ritual offers a sacred space to create a channel of devotion and communication with your chosen deity. This is a safe place where you can show up honestly, ask for help, and build a relationship with your higher power or whatever energy feels supportive to you right now.

Materials Needed

Candle (white for purity and clarity or green for healing) and a means to light it

Piece of paper and pen

Small bowl of water (symbolizing emotional depth and cleansing)

Herbs for strength and clarity such as rosemary, eucalyptus, lemon balm, and spearmint

Piece of amethyst

The Spell

+ Cleanse yourself and the area around your Sobriety Altar with the smoke of your chosen herbs or a selenite wand.
+ Take a few deep breaths, inhaling light and positivity, exhaling any negativity or doubt.
+ Visualize yourself being connected to the earth and the Universe.

+ As you light the candle, say: "I open my heart to the wisdom of my higher power. I come to you seeking clarity and guidance."

+ On the piece of paper, write down your intention to turn your will and life over to your higher power. Be specific about what that means for you in your recovery journey. Write whatever comes to mind and feels right to you. If you need some inspiration, *I surrender my fears and trust my journey of healing and sobriety* is a great place to begin.

+ Hold your hands over the bowl of water and say: "Water, cleanse my spirit and emotions. With every drop, I let go and embrace the support of my higher power."

+ Sprinkle the herbs into the water as you say: "Herbs of strength and clarity, guide me on my path and help me let go of what no longer serves me."

+ Sit quietly, focusing on the candle flame and the bowl of water. Visualize yourself surrounded by love and support from your higher power. Feel the weight of your burdens lifting as you surrender your will.

+ Fold the piece of paper and hold it high over the candle flame just enough to warm it. (Be careful not to let it catch fire or to burn yourself! If it does ignite, drop it into the water.) As the edges singe, say: "I release this intention into the Universe, trusting in the process and my higher power."

+ Place the paper on your Sobriety Altar for a full moon cycle and then dispose of it.

+ Once you feel ready, safely extinguish the candle.

+ Allow the water to sit overnight, then pour it outside (preferably at the base of your favorite tree or plant), releasing your intentions into the earth.

+ Keep the crystal with you or place it on your Sobriety Altar as a reminder of your commitment to your recovery journey and your acceptance of support from a higher power.

Repeat this spell whenever you feel the need to reconnect with your intentions or when you're facing challenges in your sobriety journey. It could feel really supportive to do this daily or weekly at first, and then make it a monthly ritual—whatever it is you need to feel grounded and connected to your higher power. Remember that recovery is a continuous process and it's good to seek guidance and support along the way.

A SPELL FOR STEP THREE: EMBRACING SURRENDER

— ◇ —

Step three asks us to turn our will and our lives over to the care of a power greater than ourselves. But surrender isn't a one-time decision—it's a practice, a spiritual muscle we build over time. This spell is a gentle ritual to help you connect with your higher power and open your heart to the transformative energy of letting go. In this sacred space, you are invited to release fear, soften resistance, and welcome in divine guidance. Let this be a moment of trust, tenderness, and devotion to your recovery.

Materials Needed

Small red candle (symbolizing strength and courage) and a means to light it

Crystals that feel helpful to you, such as amethyst for sobriety or clear quartz for clarity (optional)
Piece of paper and pen
Small bowl of water

The Spell

✦ Take a moment to center yourself. Close your eyes, take a few deep breaths, and focus on your intention to connect with your higher power and understand the importance of surrender in your recovery.

- Light the candle and place it in front of you. If you are using crystals, arrange them around the candle.
- As the flame flickers, visualize it as a guiding light to your higher power.
- On the piece of paper, write down what surrender means to you and any fears or obstacles that feel like they are blocking you from fully letting go. Be honest with yourself.
- Once you've written down your thoughts, hold the paper over the bowl of water. As you hold it, say: "Just as water flows freely, I release my fears. I surrender this to my higher power, trusting in my journey."
- Tear the paper into small pieces and drop them into the water. Visualize your fears dissolving away.
- With hands over your heart, say a small prayer or affirmation to invite your higher power into your life. Say out loud or to yourself: "Higher power, I open my heart to you. Guide me, support me, and help me understand the beauty in surrender."
- Spend a few moments in silent meditation, focusing on the flickering candle flame. Let it represent the light of your higher power, illuminating your path in recovery.
- When you feel ready, thank your higher power for the guidance and support. Extinguish the candle, symbolizing the end of the ritual but the continuation of your journey. Consider keeping the bowl of water on your Sobriety Altar as a reminder of your intentions. You may also want to journal about your experience afterward to solidify your thoughts and feelings.

Remember that embodying surrender is an ongoing process. Consider revisiting this ritual when facing resistance or discomfort as you continue on your recovery journey.

THE HIEROPHANT
AND THE LOVERS

❖ ❖ ❖

THROUGH SELF-REFLECTION,
I GA N AN UNDERSTANDING OF MY
TRUE NATURE AND UNCOVER THE
PARTS OF MYSELF TO ACCEPT
AND RELEASE WITH LOVE.

❖ ❖ ❖

When I was first learning tarot, I struggled to connect with the energy of the Hierophant and understand the card. What even is a *hierophant*, anyway?

When I finally looked it up for more context, I discovered these were priests in ancient Greece who were responsible for interpreting sacred mysteries and leading religious congregations. Basically, a hierophant receives the cosmic download and transmits it to the people. In tarot, he's the pope or the high priest who represents religious traditions, structures, and spiritual guidance. When the card is upright, it can express a desire for acceptance and approval. When the card is reversed, it can mean that someone is questioning the status quo or regulations or they are forging their own path. The idea that you need to know the rules before you can break them, as signified by the Hierophant, makes a lot of sense to me. He also represents new thinking processes and insights, which can include *acceptance*, a notion that truly stands out to me most when I consider this card.

Looking back on my sobriety journey so far, I can see that a huge turning point for me was when I embarked upon step four and "made a searching and fearless moral inventory." This step provided a path into my inner darkness, where I began shadow work (more on that shortly!) to understand why it was I was drinking and numbing out.

When I was working on this step, I often felt too sensitive—as if I were walking around with no skin. Bright lights felt harsh and loud noises always made me jump. Crowds were difficult, too. I was picking up on every nuance of every emotion of every person around me, as well as the messages of spirits who had something that needed to be heard or transmitted. My psychic abilities come through as messages, imagery, tastes, and fragrances. I can walk into a room and feel what happened there, whether it was five minutes or fifty years ago. And through a practice of self-compassion I have come to understand that this is a very intense way to live!

Now I really get why I was drinking to stop myself from feeling anything—I didn't understand how to handle so much all at once. I had to learn boundaries, both physical and energetic, and I also had to learn how to accept that this is the way I am going to live and I need to love myself in spite of the challenges it presents, even when it feels quite isolating.

Once we figure out why we are drinking or numbing out and what we are escaping, it's far easier to address *that* issue rather than putting an ineffective Band-Aid on a large wound. Through shadow work, I have also realized my immense sensitivity—something I felt so embarrassed and ashamed of—is actually one of my greatest gifts. If you also feel too sensitive at times, I hope you can come to an understanding that being sensitive is nothing to be ashamed of, it's something to accept and celebrate. My sensitivity has given me a career I love and a sense of purpose. It also makes me a better friend, partner, and family member.

Whatever it is you dislike about yourself, whatever reason you feel like you can't be present, whatever it is you have been hiding away, I hope you can look at it, explore it, be curious about it, and most importantly show it love and compassion. It's not easy to be a human, but it is a miracle to be alive, so let's commit to loving all parts of ourselves, even the ones that feel hard to love. And remember that even though making our moral inventory often brings us face to face with our fears, shame, and harm done, it's also an invitation to witness our strengths. Our resilience. Our inner magic.

This inventory isn't just a catalog of flaws; it's a mirror for the soul. When we only focus on what's broken, we miss what's beautiful. And if we're to truly transform, we need to know what we're working *with*, not just what we're working through. So yes: name your patterns. Be honest about your part. But also make space for the qualities that helped you survive: your creativity, your compassion, your insight, your loyalty, your humor. Your ability to love even when your heart was heavy.

Recovery isn't about becoming someone else; it's about returning to the truth of who you are. And that includes your goodness. Let this step be a ritual of reclamation. As you do your inventory, highlight your gifts too. You are not just your mistakes. You are also your magic.

Following the Empress and the Emperor, the Fool's Journey takes us to the Hierophant, our keeper of traditions, and the Lovers, who represent our values and choices. These figures act as a wise mentor and a pair encouraging harmony as we embark on this step and strive for self-acceptance as well as accountability.

THE HIEROPHANT

— ◇ —

Traditions, Lessons, Community,
Moral and Ethical Values

The Hierophant is associated with spirituality, tradition, and guidance. I think of this card as offering guidance through the search for meaning and connection in our lives. Spirituality and recovery go hand in hand, and this pursuit may include getting involved in spiritual practices or finding a mentor who may impart wisdom through both recovery and spirituality. The Hierophant pushes for that deeper understanding of our true nature.

It's crucial to adhere to the routines or traditions that help us maintain a sober lifestyle, and the Hierophant champions established paths and a structured environment for recovery, whether through twelve-step programs or community support. The Hierophant often suggests a connection to a community or group, which can be vital in sobriety. Being part of support groups or recovery communities fosters a sense of belonging and accountability.

The Hierophant is a spiritual leader and teacher associated with moral teachings and values. So this card can be about learning important lessons about ourselves and our relationships with others. Achieving sobriety can be a transformative education in the root causes of our addictive behavior. Our developing personal ethics around drinking and drug use can lead to a commitment to living a healthier, more responsible life.

THE LOVERS

— ◇ —

*Choices, Decisions, Self-Love and
Acceptance, Relationships, Balance,
Harmony, Duality and Integration*

The Lovers card tells us about love, relationships, choices, and duality. Its energy encourages us to consider what truly aligns with our values and long-term happiness. The harmony and balance of the Lovers suggest the need to set up a balanced lifestyle that promotes well-being and reduces the temptations associated with substance use. It may represent the conscious decision to choose a sober lifestyle over substance use. The duality of the two figures of the Lovers speaks to the integration of different aspects of oneself—acknowledging both the struggles and strengths in the recovery process. Embracing both can lead to a more holistic approach.

Sobriety offers a journey of self-discovery and self-acceptance. While the traditional step four can feel like a moment to be harsh and hard on ourselves, the Lovers card has the ability to show us the importance of *loving* ourselves—so essential for maintaining sobriety. Embracing one's true self without the influence of substances can lead to healthier personal fulfillment and interpersonal dynamics. An honest assessment of ourselves that includes identifying resentments, fears, and personal flaws is a critical step toward healing and growth, as self-reflection helps us to gain an understanding of our true natures and uncover the parts of ourselves to accept and release with love. We can always create changes, but it's as important to be able to identify what parts of ourselves we need to let go of as it is to realize what parts to integrate more fully.

Step four asks individuals to reflect on their past and present. This could be done individually, but both the Hierophant and the Lovers put a spotlight on the connection to others in our lives. This could mean working with a sponsor or attending group meetings where shared experiences provide wisdom if you are seeking a more traditional recovery route, or it could just mean seeking out sober meetups and communities to learn from others who have more experience living substance-free. There is so much value in community, and the opportunity to find sober spaces is becoming more abundant as more people question their relationship to alcohol and decide to do without. The concept of a moral inventory in sobriety will often reveal how relationships affect one's addiction and recovery. This is an opportunity to examine how our actions impact those we love and how those relationships may need to evolve.

These two cards both have an underlying message of respecting ourselves just as step four involves valuing ourselves enough to recognize and accept both our strengths and weaknesses. In sobriety we are afforded the pivotal choice to embrace growth and change. Taking an honest look at ourselves can lead to transformative decisions that align with our recovery goals. The journey of recovery calls for an ethical examination of self and a commitment to positive decision-making that honors both ourselves and others.

THE FOURS OF THE MINOR ARCANA

— ◇ —

The Fours of the Minor Arcana represent stability, reflection, and the sacred pause inviting us to build a solid foundation in sobriety, find peace in stillness, and integrate the lessons we're learning along the way.

Four of Wands
CELEBRATION AND STABILITY

This card is often associated with celebration, harmony, and a sense of community. In the context of sobriety, it can express the support system found in recovery groups, the joy of achieving milestones, and the celebration of sobriety itself every day as well as the importance of rejoicing in sober anniversaries or achievements with friends and family.

Four of Cups
REFLECTION AND REEVALUATION

This card represents contemplation and sometimes apathy. In terms of sobriety, it might indicate a period when someone is reflecting on their emotional state and deeper reasons behind their substance use. It prompts the individual to reevaluate what truly fulfills them, highlighting the importance of emotional awareness in the recovery process. It could signify a period of reflecting on past decisions and feelings crucial in step four.

Four of Swords
REST AND HEALING

This card embodies recovery, restorative practices, and taking a step back to heal. For someone in recovery, it can highlight taking time to heal mentally and emotionally, which aligns with the introspective nature of step four, while showcasing the need for self-care and rest during the recovery journey. It emphasizes the importance of mental health, reflection, and the necessity of restoring oneself after overcoming challenges.

Four of Pentacles
CONTROL AND SECURITY

This card can speak to the importance of resource management and financial stability in sobriety. Step four can involve understanding how past behaviors have impacted emotional, social, and financial resources. This card also deals with themes of control, stability, and holding on to those resources, so it could reflect the desire to secure progress and maintain the gains made in recovery. However, it can also caution against being overly controlling or resistant to change, suggesting that true security comes from openness and adaptability, not just holding on too tightly to what has been achieved.

⌣⸰⌣

Overall, the Fours in the Minor Arcana offer a multifaceted approach to concepts of stability, reflection, healing, and security crucial in the context of sobriety. They remind individuals on this journey of the importance of building a supportive community, taking time for introspection and recovery, and finding a balance between control and openness to change. Each card can serve as a guide to navigate different aspects of the sobriety journey, highlighting both the challenges and the rewards of this path.

The foundational stability of the Fours ties into the concept of step four's moral inventory leading to self-acceptance through pause and reflection. Just as the Fours represent stability, step four is about building a solid foundational awareness of our behaviors and patterns. Overall, these Four cards can collectively emphasize introspection, celebration of progress, understanding of oneself, and building a stable base during the recovery journey.

SHADOW WORK
FOR SOBRIETY

— ◇ —

Sometimes the aspects of ourselves we despise the most can alchemize into our most treasured traits. All we need is an infusion of love—often far easier said than done.

Loving ourselves is a process—just like shadow work itself. We will not find resolution overnight, but step-by-step, we will get there. And the benefits are something we can start to feel along the way. The Lovers, the Hierophant, and the Fours of the Minor Arcana offer energetic support for engaging in shadow work and uncovering why we have been drinking and using drugs.

Shadow work is a concept rooted in psychology, particularly in the ideas put forth by Swiss psychiatrist Carl Jung. It refers to the process of exploring and integrating the "darker" aspects of oneself: the traits, desires, and impulses individuals might reject or repress because they perceive them as negative or undesirable. The shadow encompasses all the parts of our personality we might not be consciously aware of, including fears, insecurities, and instincts.

Shadow work involves confronting these hidden aspects of the self, understanding their origins, and ultimately integrating them into a more complete and authentic sense of self. Doing this type of work helps us to uncover the parts of ourselves we may deem unlovable so we can show them the love they deserve. By facing and integrating these parts of ourselves, we can open a gateway to peace and self-love.

Through shadow work, we get to know ourselves better and attain greater self-awareness by realizing the motivations for our behavior. We release negative emotions and patterns that stem from unacknowledged fears or traumas, paving the path to ultimate healing. And most importantly, we learn self-acceptance through embracing all parts of ourselves, leading to greater authenticity and wholeness.

There are so many different ways to approach shadow work, but most techniques include journaling, meditation, dream analysis, and artistic expression as an entry point, sometimes alongside therapy. Because this work can sometimes bring up intense emotions and memories, I think it's helpful to take a gentle approach with support in place. It's not easy to face ourselves wholly and completely, but the tools of sobriety encourage us to do these hard things for our own benefit and greater good. While this practice can be challenging, it also offers a powerful means of personal transformation and self-acceptance—two essentials in sobriety.

The goal of shadow work is not to eliminate our darker aspects but to accept and understand them. By examining our past experiences, behaviors, triggers, and the emotional responses that may contribute to unhealthy patterns, we can recognize the root causes of our issues and work toward healing while fostering resilience. By acknowledging and integrating these shadow aspects, we can transform negative energy into a source of strength, wisdom, and creativity. This is truly an act of healing and empowerment through achieving better balance. Ultimately, we have the power to take control of our lives and invoke change because we are not our pasts or our traumas: we are our healing.

A TAROT SPREAD FOR CLARITY, EASE, AND SUPPORT DURING SHADOW WORK

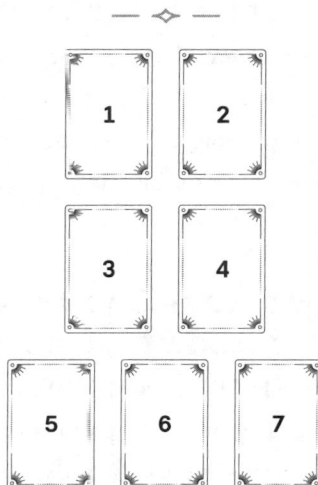

— ◇ —

```
┌─────┐   ┌─────┐
│     │   │     │
│  1  │   │  2  │
│     │   │     │
└─────┘   └─────┘

┌─────┐   ┌─────┐
│     │   │     │
│  3  │   │  4  │
│     │   │     │
└─────┘   └─────┘

┌─────┐ ┌─────┐ ┌─────┐
│     │ │     │ │     │
│  5  │ │  6  │ │  7  │
│     │ │     │ │     │
└─────┘ └─────┘ └─────┘
```

Shadow work is not easy, but when we commit to the hard work, we uncover what we need to face and create opportunities to learn, grow, and attain peace. It's worth the challenges! But it's important to show ourselves kindness and grace as we move through the process.

Sometimes the hardest part is just beginning and figuring out where that could be. I created this tarot spread to help you find the starting point and do so with love.

Card 1

WHAT ASPECT OF MY SHADOW AM I READY TO FACE?

This card provides a compass to direct you to the aspects of your shadow you are prepared to contend with. This will be the best place to focus your attention right now because you are ready.

Card 2

WHAT IS BLOCKING ME
FROM FACING THIS ASPECT
OF MY SHADOW?

This card uncovers the inherent blocks inhibiting you from seeing this aspect of your shadow. This could also provide useful information to clarify old stories you have told yourself and limitations you unknowingly placed on yourself so you can assess them and let them go.

Card 3

HOW DOES THIS ASPECT OF
MY SHADOW CURRENTLY
MANIFEST IN MY LIFE?

This card acknowledges that the darkness can be tricky to navigate and perhaps this aspect of your shadow has affected more than you previously recognized. By seeing the bigger picture or a hidden root, you can more clearly articulate its influence, putting yourself on the path to acceptance.

Card 4

WHAT CAN I LEARN FROM THIS
ASPECT OF MY SHADOW?

This card highlights the light in the dark, the silver lining: anything that challenges us or brings us pain can also offer a helpful lesson. This is what you can learn from this aspect of yourself.

Card 5

HOW CAN I SHOW THIS ASPECT
OF MY SHADOW MORE LOVE?

This card reveals an actionable step you can take to support or strengthen your bond with your shadow through acceptance and care.

Card 6
HOW CAN I CELEBRATE
AND INTEGRATE THIS ASPECT OF
MY SHADOW INTO MY LIFE?

This card shows how to incorporate the shadow into your life, guided by love, compassion, and understanding.

Card 7
HOW CAN I SHOW MYSELF
MORE CARE AS I INTEGRATE THIS
ASPECT OF MY SHADOW?

This card offers support through additional self-care to balance out the challenges of personal excavation and deep work.

A STEP FOUR
RECOVERY TAROT SPREAD

— ◇ —

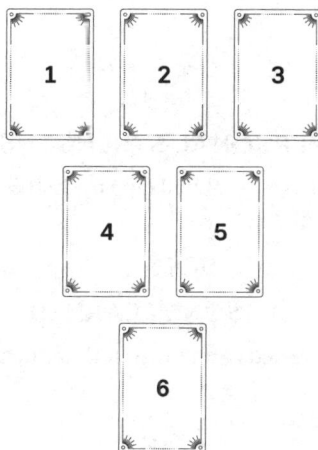

This tarot spread offers an opportunity for an honest examination and reflection of past behavior and character flaws to identify areas for growth and change. By identifying these thoughts and emotions, you can gain a deeper understanding of yourself and your patterns leading to the potential for positive transformation.

Card 1
PAST BEHAVIORS

What are some of the patterns or behaviors from my past I need to acknowledge?

Card 2
CURRENT INFLUENCE

What influences are these past behaviors currently having in my life?

Card 3
ATTRIBUTES TO RELEASE

What negative attributes or beliefs should I release to move forward in my recovery?

Card 4
PERSONAL STRENGTHS

What strengths do I possess that will help me in this process?

Card 5
LESSONS LEARNED

What lessons have I learned from my past that can aid my growth?

Card 6
NEXT STEPS

What next steps am I taking to create a positive change in my life?

Before you begin, take a moment to ground yourself. Focus on your intention for this spread and the work of checking in and taking a moral inventory. As you shuffle, think about the questions and how they relate to your recovery process. Lay out the cards as indicated and take your time interpreting each one in the context of the question it represents. Consider both the imagery and the meanings associated with the card. Write down your interpretations and any emotions or thoughts that arise through this process. After interpreting the cards, spend some time reflecting on the insights gained. You might want to write a few sentences about how you can integrate these lessons into your recovery process.

MIRROR WORK: A RITUAL TO SEE YOURSELF FULLY AND EMBODY STEP FOUR

Mirror work can be a powerful practice for self-reflection, affirmation, and healing, especially in the context of shadow work. You are beautiful—all of you—and this ritual is designed to help you to see yourself fully.

Materials Needed

Small hand mirror or a larger mirror where you can see your full reflection
Two candles (one black for letting go, one white for healing) and a means to light them

Crystals such as amethyst for sobriety support or clear quartz for amplification (optional)
Piece of paper and pen
A firesafe container (optional)

The Spell

+ For this ritual, find a quiet, comfortable place to work. Set up your mirror, candles, and any crystals you may want to use.

+ Place the candles safely near the mirror with the black candle to your left and the white candle to your right. Light the black candle first, stating, "I release my shame, freeing myself from its grasp." Then light the white candle, saying, "I embrace healing and acceptance within myself."

+ Set your intention by pausing a moment to center yourself. Close your eyes and take several deep breaths. Repeat to yourself: "I seek truth within myself; I embrace my journey of recovery." On the piece of paper, write down your responses to the following prompts. Allow yourself to be honest and open.

    * What actions or behaviors have I engaged in that have hurt myself and others?
    * What fears do I carry with me?
    * What regrets weigh on my heart?
    * What destructive patterns can I see in my behavior?

+ Once you have finished writing, take a moment to reflect on your answers. When you are ready, hold the paper in your hands and look into the mirror. Begin speaking to your reflection softly with these affirmations:

    * "I acknowledge my past and the lessons it has taught me."
    * "I am deserving of forgiveness and healing."
    * "I release my guilt and embrace the opportunity for growth."
    * "I see myself as I am, and I choose to change."

+ As you speak, notice your feelings, thoughts, and reactions. Allow yourself to fully experience this moment of honesty and vulnerability.

+ When you feel ready, take the piece of paper and hold it to your heart. Close your eyes and visualize each of the actions or emotions you've written down, transforming them into lessons that you are now ready to release. This is an act of self-forgiveness.

+ When you are ready, you can choose to carefully burn the paper in the candle flame (if it's safe to do so), representing the release of past actions and the acceptance of your journey. As you watch it burn, say out loud: "I release this past to the Universe; I embrace my future with love and strength." Another great option is to rip it up.

+ Once you feel a sense of completion, close the ritual by taking a few moments to sit in silence, inhaling deeply and exhaling any lingering negativity. Thank yourself for the work you've done today. Snuff out the candles, signifying the end of the ritual but the beginning of your renewed journey in sobriety.

Repeat this mirror work regularly, perhaps weekly or monthly, adding new insights to your inventory and affirmations. This practice will facilitate ongoing self-awareness and personal growth as you continue in recovery. Remember that recovery is a journey, and being gentle with yourself is key. Engaging in this ritual can help you embrace your past while empowering you to move forward positively.

5

THE CHARIOT AND STRENGTH

✦ ✧ ✦

BY COMMITTING TO RADICAL
HONESTY WITH MYSELF, I FIND
MY TRUE FORTITUDE AND CONTINUE
TO MOVE FORWARD ON MY PATH.

✦ ✧ ✦

The Universe will always show us signs we are on the right path and encourage us to move forward with newfound clarity. On the press preview day for my latest curated exhibition, I happened to poke my head out of my space at the exact moment a tall, familiar figure was walking down the hallway. "Is that Erik Foss?!" I called out, knowing full well there was no one else it could be. Erik owned the coolest nightclub in the East Village: Lit. When I lived on the Jersey Shore, a day off from my job at an art gallery was rare, and a night off from my second gig checking IDs and handing out shoes at the rock and roll music venue/bowling alley even rarer, but when I could get away, I would venture to Manhattan to drink with my friends at Lit.

I met Erik at my night gig on one of his rare nights away from the city. I had taken psychedelic mushrooms before coming into work. It seemed like a good idea at the time because we were hosting a music festival. All I knew about Erik was that he was an artist, he was sober, and he had helped many people excel in both arenas. I brought him a Coke from behind the bar as I told myself to keep it together. It felt supremely embarrassing to be high on psychedelics at work in front of someone who owned a nightclub and was totally sober. I had always admired Erik's sobriety from afar. How incredible to be sober, to work in nightlife, and to appear to have a life full of fun experiences and creative expression. Did he have to give anything up to live this way? In my eyes, he had it all. I remember sitting in the corner of his bar one night sipping a cocktail as I watched him drink a soda and thinking that if he could be sober and out in a bar, if he could enjoy live music and art without drinking, maybe, just maybe, I could too.

I couldn't believe I was looking at Erik Foss in the daylight. He turned around, smiled, and waved. "*Heyyyyyy*, what are you doing here, Jersey Girl?"

"I just moved here. And I curated this show: come in and see it. By the way, I'm sober now, too."

"Incredible! I closed the club and I'm making art full-time now, so I have more time to myself. You should come over and see what I'm working on."

Sobriety was allowing me to meet new people and make new friends, but it was also allowing me to reconnect with old ones.

When Erik invited me over, I realized I didn't know how to have fun now that I didn't do drugs or drink alcohol. I was prone to immersing myself in my work to keep out of trouble. I had done this when I was drinking, and I continued to rely on this tactic in my newfound sobriety. But when you're ready to change everything, you must change everything. And there's more to life than just endlessly working. We need free time, enjoyment, and pleasure that enhances and balances out our lives, rather than always numbing or distracting ourselves—or even worse, acting self-destructively. This was an opportunity to try something different; nearly anything would be better than my past choices. It can be overwhelming and daunting, or you can approach it with curiosity, wonder, and excitement. I didn't have much extra money at the time, but what I learned, even in a city as wildly expensive as Manhattan, is that fun can be had anywhere as long as you commit to creating it.

As spring blossomed in NYC, I would meet Erik and his sweet black lab Lucy (short for Lucifer) in Tompkins Square Park, where we would sit on a bench to people-watch and talk about everything. Lucy loved people but despised other dogs. She could observe them from afar but didn't want to interact with them. I wasn't ready to interact with many folks either, but being in close proximity made me feel less alone. Lucy and I were on the same wavelength.

I've always been very guarded and prone to asking questions of others while maintaining a healthy distance myself. I think this stems from feeling uncomfortable sharing my immense sensitivity with others— especially my psychic abilities, which always seemed ripe for rejection and misunderstanding. This time at the park spent telling stories and listening to Erik helped me become far more comfortable expressing myself.

"Can I tell you something I feel kind of ashamed of and totally embarrassed about? It's from the past, but I want to tell you now," I proclaimed out of nowhere as I looked straight ahead into the chaos of the park.

"Sure—this is going to be good!" Erik smiled with a devilish twinkle in his eye.

"The first time I met you, when you came to the Lanes for All Tomorrow's Parties, I was on mushrooms. I was tripping and trying so hard to hold it together in front of you because I knew I shouldn't be high at work, and you owned a nightclub and must've thought it was so embarrassing to see an employee of a club high on the job. I felt so guilty because I knew you were sober and I didn't want to look so irresponsible and dumb in front of you. I kept messing things up. I got you a Diet Coke even though you asked for a Coke, and oh my god, I can't believe I'm telling you this! It's silly, but I feel so bad about it."

"That's it? I didn't know you were high, and why would I care anyway? That's not so bad, but if you want to talk about taking psychedelics in random places, let me tell you about the time I took acid at Disneyland..."

That conversation with Erik is pretty tame compared to all of the regrettable mistakes I have made throughout my life, but it was still an important lesson. Once we start admitting to ourselves the ways we have messed up and show ourselves forgiveness, kindness, and compassion, it's easier to own it all, make apologies when necessary, and still love ourselves despite our misguided actions and screwups. Loving ourselves is a crucial part of healing and living substance-free. I don't love that traditional twelve-step programs emphasize what we have done *wrong* and the surrounding shame. When doing more traditional amends, we keep looking backward as the shameful addict. I don't know if that's helpful in enhancing self-love. Shame happens when we feel inferior, inadequate, and less than. It's crucial to do what we can to let go of these heavy negative feelings. It's incredibly important to own our mistakes and be aware of our actions and their impact, but it's also key to acknowledge that perhaps we were doing our best even though it wasn't quite good enough, forgive ourselves, and try to be better in the future.

Most people have done something inappropriate, made a mistake, or regret a past action. When we talk about these moments free of shame, we take away the power they hold over us. When we are vulnerable and share our experiences, we are often met with love and compassion. And when we love ourselves, we don't have to hold on to our mistakes so tightly.

By acknowledging and owning our past wrongs, we can move forward lighter and freer. Sometimes our little mistakes eat at us just as much as the major ones. People often assume the worst-case scenario when they imagine the destruction addicts can create: stealing from family members, driving while intoxicated, cheating on romantic partners, and the many other ways dishonesty and self-centeredness may play out.

The traditional fifth step is "Admitted the exact nature of our wrongs to a higher power, to ourselves, and to another person," and as we embark on this leg of our Fool's Journey, the cards supporting us are the Chariot, which represents the resolve we'll need to achieve that honesty, and Strength, a quality we'll need to find within ourselves along the way.

THE CHARIOT

— ◇ —

WILLPOWER, CONTROL, MOVEMENT FORWARD, BALANCE, VICTORY, AND ACHIEVEMENT

The Chariot is a card of willpower that holds a reminder of your inherent agency. You are the charioteer—and sobriety isn't the destination; it's the journey. With a commitment to sobriety, you can go anywhere and do anything you desire. Anything you can imagine is possible.

The Chariot also brings up themes of determination, control, and the victorious pursuit of goals. When considering its relation to sobriety, think of this card as a metaphor for the inner journey of overcoming addiction and navigating the challenges that arise along the way. The Chariot emphasizes discipline and personal strength. Sobriety often requires a strong commitment to overcome challenges and resist temptations. The presence of the charioteer, who must skillfully navigate the forces represented by the sphinxes, shows how we can harness our inner strength and control various influences in our lives. In the context of sobriety, the Chariot emphasizes the journey toward a healthier, more fulfilling life. It encourages us to stay focused on our recovery path and not be deterred by setbacks. The duality of the sphinxes can represent the balance between different aspects of ourselves, such as desires versus responsibilities. Achieving sobriety often requires finding a balance between our urges and the commitment to a sober lifestyle. And finally the Chariot is a symbol of triumph over obstacles: achieving sobriety can be seen as a significant victory, and this card serves as a reminder of the strength and resilience that we are cultivating throughout the journey.

STRENGTH

— ◇ —

INNER STRENGTH, COURAGE, SELF-CONTROL, INTEGRATION OF OPPOSITES, COMPASSION, PATIENCE, RESILIENCE, AND GROWTH

Sobriety requires significant inner fortitude. The Strength card encourages us to tap into our personal power and inner resources to confront challenges and make positive choices. Embracing sobriety often involves facing fears, traumas, and emotional pain. The Strength card suggests the bravery needed to tackle these issues rather than avoiding them through substance use. One of the primary aspects of maintaining sobriety is the ability to exercise self-discipline and control over urges and cravings. The Strength card highlights the importance of managing impulses and making conscious choices. It also signifies compassion—both for oneself and others. In the context of sobriety, this can mean being gentle with ourselves during the recovery process and recognizing that the journey takes time.

The traditional imagery of the Strength card—a figure calmly taming a lion—gives us an example of the integration of our instincts and desires with rational thought. In sobriety, we need to harmonize our emotional and rational sides, finding balance without resorting to substances. Recovering from addiction involves setbacks and challenges, but Strength reminds each of us of our capacity for resilience, encouraging us to view setbacks as opportunities for growth rather than failures.

THE FIVES OF THE MINOR ARCANA

— ◇ —

The Fives of the Minor Arcana each carry themes connected to challenges, inner conflicts, and potential growth.

Five of Wands
CONFLICT AND STRUGGLE

This card often represents conflict, competition, or strife. In the context of sobriety, it can point to the internal and external struggles we face while trying to overcome addiction. The chaos depicted in the card can mirror the turmoil that often accompanies the early stages of recovery, including battling cravings and disagreements with ourselves or others. However, it also suggests these conflicts can lead to growth and understanding, emphasizing the importance of channeling energy positively.

Five of Cups
GRIEVING THE LOSSES

The Five of Cups is commonly associated with loss, grief, and disappointment. For someone in recovery, this card may reflect the emotional toll of letting go of past habits, relationships, or the lifestyle associated with addiction. It highlights the importance of mourning what has been lost but also encourages recognition of the remaining possibilities and the need to focus on the future. Its theme of acceptance leads to the realization that while some things may have been lost, hope, healing, and new opportunities still exist.

Five of Swords
DEFEAT OF THE EGO

This card often signifies conflict, defeat, and the consequences of a win-at-all-costs mentality. In sobriety, the Five of Swords can represent the struggles with ego, manipulation, or toxic relationships that might hinder recovery. It serves as a reminder of the importance of choosing our battles wisely, letting go of harmful dynamics, and finding peace rather than engaging in self-sabotage or rivalry. This can be a pivotal moment to learn about humility and compassion.

Five of Pentacles
HARDSHIP OF LONELINESS

This card typically indicates feelings of lack, isolation, and hardship. It can represent the tangible struggles that may arise in sobriety, such as financial issues, loss of support, or the feeling of being outcast. Reaching out for help is essential: no one is alone on their journey. The Five of Pentacles encourages us to seek support systems and connect with others who understand our struggles.

Overall, the Fives of the Minor Arcana can be seen as a collective representation of the trials and tribulations faced during the process of sobriety. They illustrate the inner turmoil associated with facing past mistakes and the difficulties that come with being honest about them. Still, we are on a path of confronting challenges, embracing change, and seeking support while navigating the complexities of recovery, as these cards remind us. Each card encourages self-reflection and growth through that adversity, reminding us that while the journey may be difficult, it can also lead to deeper understanding, resilience, and eventual transformation. The Fives in tarot's Minor Arcana remind me that challenges are unavoidable—and maybe even necessary to move forward peacefully and contently. I can think of so many times when I used to drink rather than face my feelings in difficult situations. Sobriety has taught me that everything is temporary—including emotions—and I have the strength and resiliency to do hard things. (You do, too!)

The lessons of the Fives remind me of another pivotal moment in my first year of sobriety when I really put the lessons and new tools I was cultivating to the test. After three months of park meetups and conversations, Erik invited me to come with him and his friends to another friend's grand opening of a new bar. I hadn't been inside a bar since I stopped drinking, but the idea of going didn't sound intimidating or triggering. Maybe it was too soon to go somewhere like that, but we live in a world where alcohol is nearly everywhere. And even though I was changing so many aspects of my life, I didn't want to give up everything I loved, like live music and dancing and socializing in hidden gems at night. It was impossible to live in a trigger-free bubble, and I didn't want to anyway. So it felt like as good a time as any to face my fears and see what would happen.

The bar had a tropical theme and felt like an oasis in the city with neon lights and real plants. I was slightly on edge, yet everything was fine at our table . . . until Erik got up and stepped outside, leaving me with one of his close friends who was still a stranger to me. I have always considered myself shy and slightly strange—quirky on a good day. Alcohol always made me feel like I could be more outgoing and forget how sensitive I was to everyone's emotions . . . as well as the spirits around them who were fighting for my attention and begging to be acknowledged to transmit some sort of message. I smiled at him and looked down at my glass of water, mindlessly playing with the straw. The silence felt like it was try-ing to kill me, and I was so uncomfortable I thought this could be it. I had given sobriety a go and proved I could do it this long—but maybe this was all I had in me. The bar was just over there, and I could order a drink and end this excruciating discomfort.

But what would happen if I waited it out? This was the first time out of all my attempts at sobriety when I didn't rush to give in at the first chal-lenging moment. I thought of the Chariot and its reminder of willpower and the Five of Wands that shows us that confrontation is sometimes necessary. So what if I confronted this feeling for fifteen minutes? If it didn't go away, I could order an alcoholic beverage . . . After all, it would *only* be fifteen minutes. I decided I could do that, especially with my new exit strategy in place.

As I came to that conclusion, I could feel a brotherly presence con-nected to Erik's friend. I could tell this wasn't an actual brother but some-one who felt like a brother—a very close friend who had a tight bond with him. The messages began to come through quite clearly: *Ask him about the first girl to break his heart. Ugh, couldn't it be a lighter and less invasive ques-tion? Is that really an icebreaker?* But since I already felt weird, why not just fully embrace the moment—if I couldn't handle it, I could order a drink in fifteen minutes anyway.

"So . . . why don't you tell me about your first heartbreak?" I asked as I looked up from my drink. He immediately started laughing.

"Wow, Sarah, you get right in there, huh? I never liked small talk any-way, but you know what's so funny? My best friend always used to ask me questions like that. I miss him so much. I miss him every day. He would have loved this place. I wish he were here to see what our friends created. He was gone too soon. But anyway, let me tell you about my first heart-break. I met her when I was seventeen . . ."

I became fully engrossed in his story. Heartbreak is so relatable, and I was healing from a broken heart, too. Aren't we all? The human experience may seem like a solo journey but it's actually a shared experience. We are all basically navigating the same themes.

"What a beautiful story! Thank you for sharing that with me."

"Hey, what did I miss?" Erik was back, and I checked my phone. It was now thirty minutes later, and I no longer wanted that drink. I felt a little more at ease, and I immediately saw the benefit of doing something difficult, of facing a fear and knowing I had good friends by my side to support me when life felt challenging.

"Oh, we are just talking about our first heartbreaks . . . you're next!" I giggled. That night showed me that bars can be fun without being damaging. Anywhere is good when you're with good people. Triggers will always exist, but how we respond to them is up to us.

Together, the Chariot, Strength, and the Fives of the Minor Arcana reflect confronting our past in a sober, honest manner. They emphasize the need for control, courage, and the possibility of overcoming challenges—all essential to successfully completing step five in recovery. The Chariot shows us we can steer our life in the desired direction; we can make conscious choices to pursue sobriety and take charge of our journey. The Chariot also signifies triumph over challenges and obstacles, mirroring the struggles faced during recovery. It encourages embracing the discipline and determination essential in step five where we confront past behaviors honestly. Strength reminds us of our inner fortitude in facing our fears. This courage is vital to acknowledge and share our wrongs. The Strength card suggests that true strength lies in vulnerability and honesty with ourselves and others. Strength also embodies compassion—not only for ourselves but also for others. Making amends is about understanding how past behaviors have affected others. All of the Fives acknowledge the discomfort of facing tough issues (loss, poverty, conflict, barriers) but also highlight the potential for growth and a new path—the opportunity for transformation. In step five, acknowledging mistakes is the first move toward making positive changes.

A TAROT SPREAD TO ACKNOWLEDGE AND LET GO OF SHAME

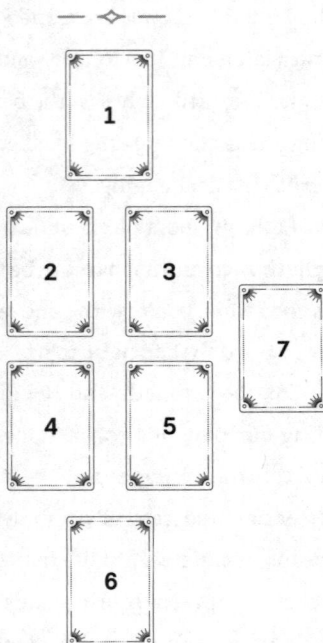

— ◇ —

```
        ┌─────┐
        │     │
        │  1  │
        │     │
        └─────┘

┌─────┐   ┌─────┐
│     │   │     │   ┌─────┐
│  2  │   │  3  │   │     │
│     │   │     │   │  7  │
└─────┘   └─────┘   │     │
                    └─────┘
┌─────┐   ┌─────┐
│     │   │     │
│  4  │   │  5  │
│     │   │     │
└─────┘   └─────┘

        ┌─────┐
        │     │
        │  6  │
        │     │
        └─────┘
```

Shame is one of the heaviest emotions we carry in recovery and one of the most important to face with compassion and curiosity. This spread is a ritual of self-inquiry and release, designed to help you gently explore the roots of your shame, understand what it's trying to teach you, and begin the process of forgiveness and letting go. Let each card be a mirror, a balm, and a guide as you reclaim your worthiness and reconnect with your inner light.

Card 1: The source of my shame

Card 2: What can I learn from my feelings of shame?

Card 3: How can I support myself right now as I process these feelings of shame?

Card 4: What do I need more of in order to help myself process these feelings?

Card 5: What do I need less of in order to help myself process these feelings?

Card 6: What do I need to help forgive myself?

Card 7: What do I need to release this feeling of shame?

A STEP FIVE TAROT SPREAD

— ◇ —

For a tarot spread focused on step five, we can aim to explore the themes of honesty, connection, vulnerability, and healing.

Card 1

THE CHALLENGE OF HONESTY

What emotional barriers or fears do I face in admitting my wrongs?

This card will help you identify any internal struggles or fears related to being honest about your past actions.

Card 2

THE VALUE OF CONNECTION

Who or what supports my journey toward admitting my truths?

This card can represent the people in your life, higher powers, or supportive communities that can aid you on this journey.

Card 3

THE PATH TO HEALING

What steps can I take to embrace honesty and move forward?

This card provides guidance or insight on how to accept your past, embrace authenticity, and foster healing in your recovery process.

After drawing the cards, take some time to reflect on their meanings and how they relate to your current recovery journey. Journaling about the insights you gain from this spread can enhance your understanding and provide further clarity on how to navigate the challenges of step five.

Approach this spread with an open heart and mind. If you're comfortable, share the insights and reflections with a trusted person as part of the process. Remember that this is a personal journey, and the insights you gain can be tailored to your unique experiences.

A TAROT SPREAD FOR FACING HARD THINGS

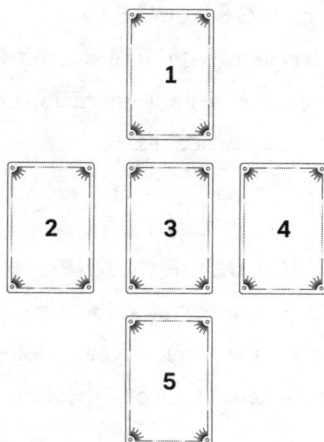

```
          +-----+
          |  1  |
          +-----+

+-----+   +-----+   +-----+
|  2  |   |  3  |   |  4  |
+-----+   +-----+   +-----+

          +-----+
          |  5  |
          +-----+
```

This is a tarot spread designed to help you face difficult situations and find the courage and clarity to take action. Sobriety has taught me that life doesn't just become easy once we stop drinking or getting high, but our resilience does increase. Our ability to keep calm and confront challenges improves because we start to learn how capable we are. We are no longer creating bigger messes or more chaos through avoidance. This spread is a powerful tool for self-reflection and empowerment, enabling you to approach difficult situations with renewed insight and confidence wherever you are in your sober journey.

Card 1
THE CHALLENGE

This card represents the specific challenge or hard situation you are facing. It highlights the nature of the difficulty and what you need to confront.

Card 2
YOUR CURRENT MINDSET

This card reflects your current mental and emotional state regarding the challenge. It reveals any fears, doubts, or beliefs that may be holding you back.

Card 3
THE PATH FORWARD

This card offers guidance on how to approach the challenge. It can provide insights, strategies, or actions you can take to move forward.

Card 4
RESOURCES AND SUPPORT

This card indicates what you can draw on to help you face this challenge. This could include internal strengths, external support systems, or tools you can utilize.

Card 5
THE OUTCOME

This card reflects the potential outcome if you face the challenge with courage and follow the guidance provided. It can offer hope and show what is possible if you take action.

⌣ ⚬ ⌣

Focus on your question or situation while shuffling the tarot deck. Draw five cards and place them in a cross, with one card at the top, three cards across, and one card at the bottom (see page 94). Reflect on each card and its position, considering the meanings and how they relate to your current challenge. Take notes on what resonates with you and how you feel about the insights provided. Reflect on the messages of the cards. Journaling about your thoughts and feelings can also help you process the information and create a plan for moving forward. After interpreting the spread, consider practical steps you can take to implement the guidance and insights gained.

A RITUAL TO PROCESS AND RELEASE SHAME (FOR PERSONAL GROWTH)

— ◇ —

Step five emphasizes admitting the exact nature of our wrongs, which can be a pivotal moment in taking accountability and fostering personal growth.

Processing and releasing shame are an important part of recovery, especially in the context of step five and looking directly at the wrongs we have done. This ritual is designed to help you understand and embody the process of admitting wrongs and foster healing and acceptance. In naming our shadow, we open our hearts to greater self-love, compassion, and acceptance.

May this ritual assist you in finding peace and freedom from shame as you journey through your recovery.

Materials Needed

Strength card from your
favorite tarot deck
Piece of paper and pen
Small bowl of water
Black candle (for protection
and absorbing negativity)
and a means to light t
A few drops of essential
oil (my suggestion is
lavender for calmness
or frankincense for
spiritual connection)

Small stone or crystal (my
suggestion is amethyst
for healing or black
tourmaline for protection)
A firesafe dish
A houseplant (If you do
not have one, I suggest
getting a snake plant,
as they are very easy to
care for and forgiving of
mistakes, which is aligned
with this particular spell!
Pothos, spider plants,
and jade plants are also
very beginner-friendly.)

The Spell

✦ Find a quiet, comfortable space where you won't be disturbed. You can light incense or play soft music if it helps you feel more relaxed and focused. Take a few deep breaths and begin to set your intentions by thinking about the meaning of the Strength card. Hold the card in your hand and allow its healing energy into your heart, opening it to vulnerability and honesty as you ask yourself some or all of the following questions. These questions are meant to encourage deep reflection and promote a sense of accountability and growth. You may wish to answer all or only some. Take what you need and leave the rest.

  ✳ What truths do I need to acknowledge?

  ✳ What am I ready to admit to myself?

* What do I feel remorse over?
* What do I fear the most about admitting my wrongs to myself and others?
* What are the specific actions or behaviors I have taken that I feel were hurtful to myself or others?
* How have my past actions affected my emotions and relationships?
* Are there recurring themes or patterns in my behavior that I have noticed? How can I address these?
* In what ways have I tried to justify or rationalize my actions instead of taking responsibility?
* Who have I harmed through my actions and in what ways?
* Have I been truly honest with myself about my shortcomings? Why or why not?
* What role does my higher power play in helping me understand and admit my wrongs?
* Who can I trust to share my admissions with, and what qualities do I seek in that person?
* How can acknowledging my wrongs contribute to my personal growth and recovery journey? What are my fears surrounding vulnerability and the potential judgment of others?
* How can I work through these fears?
* What lessons have I learned from my past mistakes, and how can I use them to make better choices moving forward?
* What steps can I take to make amends with those I have harmed?
* What might be the first step I can take?
+ On the piece of paper, write down the confessions you need to admit to yourself and to others. This might include feelings of

guilt, shame, or any mistakes you've made. This is a personal process. Be as honest and detailed as you feel comfortable with. Invite your higher power to join you and read everything out loud to them. Dip your fingers in the bowl of water and sprinkle a few drops on the paper, saying:

> "With this water, I cleanse my heart,
> From hidden secrets and shame, I choose to part.
> In truth, I find my path to grace,
> As I embrace this rightful place."

+ As you light the candle, focus on the flame. Visualize it burning away your fears and illuminating your truths. Say:

> "With this flame, I light my way,
> In honesty, I find strength today.
> Each word I share shall bring me peace,
> And in this moment, my burdens cease."

+ Put a few drops of essential oil on your stone or crystal, holding it in your hand as you meditate on your intention and say out loud:

> "This stone I hold with courage clear,
> It grounds my spirit, calms my fear.
> With every truth that comes to light,
> I step toward healing, day and night."

+ Release and surrender any lingering feelings of guilt and shame by safely burning the paper in a cauldron or firesafe dish, letting the smoke carry your words and burdens away.

+ Once the ashes have cooled, bury them in the soil of your houseplant as a way of planting new growth and healing. Express your gratitude to the plant for their support in your healing.
+ Close the ritual by thanking your higher power and reflect on the healing you've begun. Feel gratitude for your journey. Extinguish the candle, knowing that the light of honesty will continue to guide you.
+ On a fresh piece of paper, write down your answers to the following: Despite my past actions, what am I grateful for in this moment? How can that help me move forward? How can I practice self-compassion as I confront my past? What words of kindness can I offer myself?
+ Place this piece of paper somewhere you can see it every morning. This could be on your Sobriety Altar, in the corner of your mirror, or somewhere else you begin your day. Be sure to read it as part of your morning rituals.

Remember, this spell is a tool to help you embody and understand the strength, vulnerability, and honesty in step five, but the real work lies in your ongoing commitment to honesty and connection in your recovery. You are not alone on this journey, and each step you take brings you closer to healing. This spell can be repeated whenever you feel the need to reflect on your past or as a ritual to strengthen your commitment to your recovery journey.

6

THE HERMIT AND WHEEL OF FORTUNE

✧ ✦ ✧

SELF-ACCEPTANCE THROUGH SELF-DISCOVERY SUPPORTS MY INVOCATION OF CHANGE.

✧ ✦ ✧

As part of my commitment to sobriety, I knew I needed to make new friends—some who didn't drink and who I could find new ways to spend my sober time with. But where do you make friends when you work for yourself and live in a new city? You have to open yourself up to possibilities and be unafraid to try new things! Put yourself in new situations and talk to new people. If the choices you once made were bad for you, you must try something (anything!) else for different results. It helps if you notice details about people and situations, which is easier without drinking clouding your perception.

I accepted an invitation to attend a friend's art opening on Long Island. I knew I wouldn't know many people and that could be challenging to navigate without the lubricant of alcohol, but supporting a friend felt more important than giving in to my fear. I went, unsure of how it would turn out. "What's the worst that could happen?" had become a helpful sober mantra that inspired me to put myself into uncomfortable situations I previously needed a substance to endure.

I mindlessly walked around the opening, staring at each painting and sipping my seltzer, but I kept getting distracted by the sea of red wine glasses in every hand. Then I noticed one set of slender fingers clutching a bottle of sparkling water. Who was this? A glamorous, nearly six-foot-tall goddess with long blonde hair, dramatic eyeliner, and a black gown that would delight Morticia Addams. She was a force! And she was drinking water! She smiled at me; I smiled back and waved. We had both noticed each other's waters—addicts are aware of every drink in the room and how it's drunk.

"I like your dress!" she told me as she approached. "I love unicorns."

I was wearing a Samantha Pleet mini dress with a print inspired by the Unicorn Tapestries at the Cloisters. It was my favorite, and I had saved up money for months to purchase it because it reminded me of the unicorn image on my Sobriety Altar and its symbolic energy of transformation and hope. It was the first nice thing I had treated myself to since I got sober. Sometimes it seems easier to do hard things when you employ a little glamour magic to invoke feeling more powerful, even when confidence is challenging. It was meaningful to me that she noticed this detail right away.

It turned out that this woman, Anka, was an artist in the show. We chatted about unicorns and art and our birth charts, which led us to realize I had the same birthday as her mom and she had the same as my mom—a cosmic connection that made her feel immediately familiar.

"I am so happy we met tonight. I don't drink, and I was feeling nervous about coming here. I've been sober for eleven months," she told me.

My eyes lit up. She might as well have said *she* was about to turn into a unicorn. Eleven months of continuously abstaining from alcohol felt just as magical and impossible in my mind.

"I have three months alcohol-free," I whispered. "I know this might be weird, but since we both live in the city, do you want to attend a meditation with me? It's a past-life regression, and I want to go, but I don't have anyone to go with. I don't have many sober girlfriends."

"I would love to, that sounds fun!" she said. "I don't have any sober girl-friends at all."

We exchanged numbers, and that was the start of our friendship. I know that what's meant to find us always does and divine timing works in myste-rious ways. All we need to do is say yes to invitations and make good choices that align with our values, like the Lovers card reminds us to do.

I was glad to have found someone to attend the meditation with me. I'd been nervous to go alone, but it felt important—maybe there was some-thing in a past life that could show me understanding in this lifetime? Or at least it was something to do that was psychedelic but without substances.

I was about to have my answer because two weeks later, Anka and I were sitting on the floor in a windowless room of a yoga studio in a building on the Bowery awaiting our voyage to our past lives. The Lower East Side of Manhattan may not be the first place you'd think to go for a transcendent experience. If you look up, you will see fresh construction of a ten-million-dollar penthouse, and if you look down, you'll see a rat dragging a bagel to his trash-mountain home on the sidewalk (and I actually have!). As New York streets go, the Bowery is a bit grimy, but that felt far more aligned with my idea of an otherworldly interdimensional trip through time than a pristine spa in the desert or whatever social media presents as a pictur-esque place for a perfectly curated life-altering moment of wellness. You can have a magical experience anywhere, even in the grittiest of places. Healing often isn't pretty, after all.

Colorful light projections danced on the walls as the low hum of binaural beats in the restorative frequency of 528 Hz played in the background. As our fellow time travelers trailed in, the anticipation of the unknown began to build, just as it had before my first psychedelic trip as a teen on the Jersey Shore.

On the sand that day so many years ago, I had awaited the moment the mushrooms would kick in, unsure of what would happen or what I might see—I had, somewhat recklessly, taken quite a few, hoping to ensure I would skyrocket off to another dimension. I shuffled my tarot cards and gave my friends readings under the stars. I thought my readings could benefit from the addition of psychedelics, but now I realize I didn't actually need the mushrooms to get to where I was going. I already knew the path to the astral realm; the mushrooms just sped up the process to get there.

Now, attempting a sober trip, I figured, *Since I already know the route, maybe this time will be similar even without the drugs?* I was about to find out, as I was snapped back to the present moment by the tall, thin man wearing glasses and a charcoal gray suit I recognized from the sandwich board on the sidewalk as our past-life pilot for the evening. I thought, *THIS is our guide?* He had the posture of a praying mantis without the ethereal energy. His aura felt rather creepy, far from the gentle confidence I would hope to find in a chaperone for this sort of otherworldly excursion. I forced myself to put my unease aside and lay down on the yoga mat.

Our guide provided prompts to lead us into another lifetime. I was transported to a wild party where everyone was dancing, drinks were spilling, and the music was loud. It looked like a Prohibition-era speakeasy in NYC. A man smiled, lit my cigarette, popped a fresh gin martini in my hand, and grabbed my free one to pull me onto the dance floor. The cigarette dangled from my lips as I took a large sip from my drink and felt the liquor burn the back of my throat. I began to laugh as he swung me around in tune with the fast-paced music. My drink sloshed over the sides of the

104

glass, but nothing seemed to matter besides the ecstasy of the moment. I felt exhilarated, as if the night's carefree jubilance would never end.

I loved seeing this past version of myself having so much fun. But the warmth soon grew to a roaring fire and I felt the searing pain of my heart cracking into two as I realized I would never experience fun like that again, drinking and smoking and dancing all night long, losing all sense of time and reality on the dance floor of a secret nightclub. Tears welled up in my eyes and cascaded down my cheeks, accompanied by body-shaking wails. The happy scene disintegrated in front of my eyes, and I was on the floor of the yoga studio sobbing uncontrollably as the weight of sobriety work kicked in and I realized the old me was slipping away. That version of me was dying, and the heavy realization that I had to let her go brought tidal waves of grief.

The facilitator looked at me and quickly and wordlessly backed away and left the room. Had he never seen an emotional response like mine? How could someone lead me to that place and then abandon me? Sometimes a guide in our healing is simply the person holding up the mirror for us, and it doesn't mean they have any additional power we don't possess. They merely show us what already exists within us. The journey is ours alone, and we are our own guides. But still, his reaction felt irresponsible and reminded me that healing spaces aren't always safe ones, but listening to your intuition (I *knew* something was off about him!) and surrounding yourself with kind, compassionate, and understanding people make traversing the wild journey of healing so much easier, even if it is often a solo mission.

Anka, a caring Cancer Sun with a Cancer Moon (*also* just like my mom!), threw her arms around me without hesitation and hugged me until I could catch my breath again and my tears subsided. Dying is hard, but living is harder, and I was now ready to embody my choice to live. Like the Hermit card, I was navigating through the darkness guided by my own inner light. It was hard to see where I was headed. I remembered (as the Wheel of

Fortune teaches us) that the only constant is change, and I *must* change. Standing still—or worse, going backward—was simply not an option. I thought I was already doing something difficult by giving up drinking and drugs, but now I was ready to do something even more difficult: my recovery was in my hands, and it was time to give up that old party girl identity. Sometimes you have to let a version of yourself die so you can be reborn into someone new.

Step six is the readiness to accept transformation—traditionally, "Became willing to collaborate with a higher power to transform all these defects of character." I was ready to transform, but I had to figure out who I was becoming.

THE HERMIT
— ◇ —

Self-Reflection, Isolation and Solitude, Guidance
and Wisdom, Spiritual Growth, Patience and Time

Whenever I get a new tarot deck, I like to spend time with the Hermit to see how the artist depicts his light source. To me, that is the most significant aspect of the card. A formidable solitary presence, the Hermit, usually cloaked, is forging into the darkness illuminated by a light source symbolic of inner wisdom and intuition.

The Hermit is associated with introspection, solitude, and inner guidance. He encourages individuals to look inward as he symbolically shows us the essential journey into the self often necessary for achieving and maintaining sobriety. He highlights themes of self-awareness, guidance, and personal growth. In the context of sobriety, this introspection can lead to a deeper understanding of our relationship with substances or habits. It invites us to examine the motivations and feelings that may have driven previous behaviors. The Hermit's path is one of solitude. While solitude can sometimes feel isolating, it can also provide valuable time for healing and clarity crucial in the recovery journey. This solitude allows us to distance ourselves from external distractions and societal pressures that may have contributed to substance use.

The Hermit carries the lantern of wisdom, which can represent seeking guidance from within or from trusted mentors or support systems. This wisdom can help us navigate our recovery more effectively. The sobriety journey is often spiritual, and the Hermit emphasizes the importance of this connection. We may find that embracing a spiritual path—be it through tradition, nature, or personal belief—can aid in maintaining sobriety and finding peace. The Hermit reminds us that the recovery journey is not about rushing to a destination; it's a process that requires patience and acknowledgment of our unique pace to find healing and stability.

THE WHEEL OF FORTUNE

— ◇ —

Cycles of Life, Change and Transformation,
Karma and Accountability

The Wheel of Fortune card is rich in symbolism representing change, fate, and the inevitable ups and downs of life. This card suggests that life is full of cycles, including periods of struggle and periods of upward motion. In sobriety, this can remind us that cravings or challenges are often temporary. It emphasizes the importance of patience and resilience in the recovery journey. The Wheel of Fortune is also about change and the possibility of a new direction. In recovery this can be the opportunity to break free from past patterns of addiction and embrace a new, healthier lifestyle. Change *is* possible, and we have the power to influence our destinies.

The Wheel of Fortune also serves as a reminder that not everything is within our control. It represents how life can bring unexpected shifts, much like the unexpected challenges of sobriety. The key lesson here is to be adaptable and navigate these changes without reverting to old habits. The Wheel of Fortune introduces the concept of karma, or the idea that our actions have consequences. In the context of sobriety, this brings up the importance of taking responsibility for our actions and choices and recognizing how past behaviors can influence the present and future. Ultimately, the Wheel of Fortune can serve as a symbol of hope. Even if you face setbacks or difficult times in recovery, this card signals that better times are ahead and perseverance can lead to positive outcomes.

Together, the Wheel of Fortune and the Hermit illustrate the journey of recovery and personal growth. The interplay of these two cards suggests that as we reflect on our life's cycle and learn from our experiences, we can prepare to let go of what no longer serves us.

THE SIXES OF THE MINOR ARCANA

The Sixes in the Minor Arcana each emphasize themes of reflection, support, transition, and success, all of which can play vital roles in the journey of sobriety. Each card speaks to different aspects of healing and personal growth, encouraging us to embrace our journey with hope and resilience.

Six of Wands
RECOGNITION OF
HARD WORK PAYING OFF

This card expresses victory, recognition, and achievement. In terms of sobriety, the Six of Wands can signal milestones and successes—celebrating victories, both big and small, on the sober journey. It reinforces that perseverance and hard work can lead to triumph and reminds us acknowledging progress is essential. This card encourages us to take pride in our achievements and to recognize the strength shown in overcoming difficulties.

Six of Cups
JOY AND SIMPLICITY IN SOBRIETY

This card is often about nostalgia, childhood memories, and innocence. In the context of sobriety, it can show us the importance of reconnecting with our true self or revisiting joyful, simpler times that may have been overshadowed by addiction. It encourages us to cultivate a sense of joy and to reflect positively on our past, perhaps finding strength and inspiration from happy memories to support our sober journey.

Six of Swords
LEAVE THE PAST BEHIND TO
EMBRACE NEW BEGINNINGS

The Six of Swords signifies transition, movement, and change. This may be the journey away from troubled waters (symbolic of addiction and struggles) toward a calmer, stabler state. This Six embodies the idea of moving forward and leaving behind the past, emphasizing the journey itself and the transformations that occur along the way. While the path to sobriety may be challenging, it can also lead to a more peaceful and fulfilling existence.

Six of Pentacles
GIVE AND RECEIVE HELP AND SUPPORT

This card embodies the themes of giving and receiving, balance, and generosity. In sobriety, it highlights the importance of support systems—both giving and receiving help from others. It may indicate the value of community and the role that mentorship and helping others can play in recovery. It encourages us to find balance in our lives and suggests that sharing our experiences can foster healing for both the giver and the receiver.

The sixth step involves becoming entirely ready to have one's character defects removed. Both the Wheel of Fortune and the Hermit promote the notion of self-awareness and the willingness to change, essential components in the character transformation of sobriety.

Step six is the halfway point in the journey through the steps, and Sixes in tarot are a part of the halfway point through the story of each Minor Arcana. Sixes provide a place to regain our balance after the turmoil and conflict of the Fives. A Six arises with memories when a querent is feeling nostalgic. It's a time to reflect on how far we've come and to process events from our past we were previously unable to look at without some distance. How do we view the past through the lens of where we currently are?

A TAROT SPREAD FOR BECOMING THE NEXT VERSION OF YOURSELF

1	2	3
4	5	6

This tarot spread is designed to help you see who you were and who you are becoming through your beautiful transformation of sobriety. Every version of ourselves exists within us, but sometimes it's easier to know where we are going or who we are becoming if we have a little direction!

Card 1: Who I was

Card 2: Who I am currently

Card 3: Who I will ideally become

Card 4: What do I need to release?

Card 5: What do I need to embrace?

Card 6: Advice/support to transform

A STEP SIX
TAROT SPREAD

— ◇ —

```
┌─────┐  ┌─────┐
│  1  │  │  2  │
└─────┘  └─────┘

┌─────┐  ┌─────┐
│  3  │  │  4  │
└─────┘  └─────┘

┌─────┐
│  5  │
└─────┘
```

Step six invites us into a sacred moment of readiness, a willingness to release the patterns, behaviors, and defenses that no longer serve us. This spread helps illuminate the deeper roots of our character defects, the emotional currents beneath them, and the path forward toward healing and growth. Use this reading as a tool for self-awareness, spiritual preparation, and transformation as you step into the next phase of your recovery with courage and clarity.

Card 1
WHAT ARE MY CURRENT DEFECTS OF CHARACTER?

This card will shed light on the traits or habits you may be struggling with or wish to change.

Card 2
WHAT EMOTIONS OR BELIEFS CONTRIBUTE TO THESE DEFECTS?

This card will help you understand the underlying feelings or convictions that may be driving these behaviors.

Card 3,
WHAT IS STANDING IN THE WAY OF MY WILLINGNESS TO CHANGE?

This card will reveal any fears, doubts, or resistances you may have about the process of change.

Card 4
WHAT SUPPORT OR RESOURCES DO I HAVE AVAILABLE?

This card will indicate the strengths, support systems, or opportunities you can draw upon during this process.

Card 5
WHAT IS THE POTENTIAL POSITIVE OUTCOME OF EMBRACING THIS CHANGE?

This card will provide insight into the benefits and transformations that may come from letting go of these defects.

A SPELL TO EASE THE UNKNOWN AND FEEL EMPOWERED THROUGH TRANSFORMATION

— ◇ —

When a caterpillar creates their cocoon, do they know what they will look like when they emerge? The patterns and colors of their wings? Or where those wings will take them? All they know is that they can't stay a caterpillar any longer and they must transform into the new version of themselves. I created the Butterfly Transforming Spray to transfigure the fears around what's next into the excitement of potential adventure. Spray yourself and your space liberally and prepare to ascend into the next greatest version of yourself.

Materials Needed

A means to play music
Paper and pen
Six chips of citrine
Dropper of rubbing alcohol
4 drops of frankincense
3 drops of clary sage
3 drops of orange
3 drops of geranium
3 drops of palo santo
3 drops of Roman chamomile
3 drops of ylang-ylang
A 4 oz. spray bottle
Moon water (see
recipe on p. 114)

The Spell

✦ Listen to "Landslide" by Fleetwood Mac. When Stevie sings "Well, I've been 'fraid of changin'...," think about the changes you fear. Write them all down.

✦ Add the crystals, rubbing alcohol, and essential oils to the spray bottle, and then decant moon water with a funnel to where the bottle begins to curve to the neck (nearly full but not quite) and cap before giving a good shake.

✦ Hold the bottle in your hands and read your list aloud as you picture all the transformations you will embark upon. Stay in this moment as long as necessary to infuse this intention into your spray.

✦ Fold the slip of paper three times and place it beneath the bottle on your altar or windowsill. Enchant for one full moon cycle.

✦ Spray yourself, your energetic field, and your space to assist and support your transformation.

How to Make Moon Water

Moon water is simply water that has been charged under the light of the moon. It's a gentle, powerful way to work with lunar energy—to infuse your spiritual practice with intention, intuition, and a little bit of magic. You can use moon water for cleansing, spellwork, watering your plants, anointing your altar, or even just sipping it as a sacred reminder of your connection to something greater. (Only drink moon water if you've used safe, clean water and no added herbs or crystals.)

✦ To make it, all you need is a jar or bowl of water (glass is best) and a clear intention. Set the container outside or on a windowsill overnight during the full moon or any moon phase that feels aligned for you.

✦ You might want to place crystals around your jar or bowl.

✦ Speak your intentions into the water: whisper a prayer or a hope, or write a wish and tuck it beneath the jar.

✦ In the morning, thank the moon and bring your water inside. You've just made a little lunar potion, one that holds the energy of where you are, what you're calling in, and what you're ready to honor.

AWAKENING TO TRANSFORMATION: A RITUAL FOR STEP SIX OF RECOVERY

— ◇ —

In this ritual we'll focus on releasing old patterns, habits, and energies that no longer serve you, making way for new growth and transformation.

Materials Needed

Paper and pen
Incense (my preference for this spell is frankincense)

Butterfly Transformation Spray

The Spell

✦ Select a quiet, peaceful space for your ritual. Set an intention by writing down what you want to release and transform within yourself. This could be a specific habit, emotional pattern, or aspect of your character.

✦ Take a few deep breaths, feeling the earth beneath your feet. Visualize roots growing from the soles of your feet, deep into the ground, anchoring you in stability and calm.

✦ Light your incense to represent purification. As you inhale the scent, imagine any impurities, doubts, or fears leaving your body.

+ Mist the Butterfly Transformation Spray in the air around you or directly on your skin. Imagine it dissolving any remaining blockages, stagnant energies, or patterns that no longer serve you.
+ Hold your written intention in your hand. As you read it, reflect on the emotions and thoughts associated with this aspect of yourself that you want to transform.
+ Visualize a bright light surrounding you, filling any spaces within your body and energy field where the old patterns reside. Imagine these energies releasing, dissolving like mist in the sun. As you exhale, imagine fresh, vibrant energy entering your being, filling any spaces left by the released patterns. Visualize this new energy infusing into your cells, nourishing your mind, body, and spirit.
+ Take a few moments to acknowledge the transformation that has occurred within you.
+ Seal this new energy with a gentle touch on your heart or third eye center.
+ Take a final deep breath, feeling grounded and renewed.
+ Offer gratitude for this process and the courage to let go of what no longer serves you.

Continue to use your energy spray whenever you need a reminder of your intentions.

7

JUSTICE AND THE HANGED MAN

✧ ✧ ✧

HUMBLY ASKING FOR HELP
OFFERS A NEW PERSPECTIVE.

✧ ✧ ✧

"I think you need a reading," my new friend Cody announced matter-of-factly. A series of magical happenstances had aligned in order for us to meet, and now I was sitting at her kitchen table as she made us popcorn on the stove in her Hudson Valley home.

With all the newfound time I had on my hands in early sobriety, I'd made a commitment to try new things and go to new places even if it scared me, and I found myself encountering enchantment and delighting in discovery more and more. I had heard about an art exhibition by Jesse Bransford exploring esoteric symbolism through art pieces that effectively acted like spells to create the effects promised by their titles, like *To Receive All You Ask For* and *To Protect Trees*. The exhibition was on display at the estate of Kurt Seligmann, an occultist and surrealist who wrote extensively on the relationship between art and the unconscious mind. I had heard rumors that he enchanted his paints and brushes through magical rituals and even hosted occult rituals in his Sugar Loaf home for an array of vibrant guests. What a dream! Something was pulling me to this place; I knew there was something I needed there, and I was getting more comfortable saying yes to my intuition again.

Immediately upon my arrival at the estate, I was greeted by Olivia, the director of the museum, who appeared to be around my age. "I am sure you've heard of all of the magic that happens here," she said with a knowing twinkle in her eye as she brought me to the exhibition housed in Kurt's former studio. On our walk of the property, she pointed to a small hole in the barn door. "According to the legends of this home, that's a bullet hole that resulted from a heated debate between Seligmann and fellow Surrealist Max Ernst over the meaning of tarot's Fool card . . ." I loved it here!

As I stepped inside, I felt a powerful shift in the energy, an inviting magnetic pull. I could sense that incredible, transformative happenings began and blossomed here. The room was spacious and the ceilings soared high above us, supported by wooden beams that framed floor-to-ceiling glass panels allowing the natural beauty of the estate's flora and fauna to become part of the space. Jesse's artwork felt immediately at home here, with the intricate linework and layered geometric patterns in muted tones evoking sigils exploring the realm of the mystical and hidden. They were quiet, yet active.

My eyes immediately zeroed in on the large magic circles adorning the floor. Now *these* were spells! Something truly enchanting had happened here, over and over again. I knew I was exactly where I was meant to be. My thoughts were interrupted by Olivia's voice: "You must meet Cody. Let me see if she's available; she works in the office, too."

Moments later, a woman with curly red hair and an infectious smile joined us. The three of us sat within the confines of the magical circles drawn on the floor and hours were lost as they regaled me with supernatural stories of the property that felt almost too surreal to be true yet too compelling not to be. Magic is real, and that afternoon with these women reminded me of that. I told them about the recent turns my life had taken, how I was in my first year of sobriety, how my art advising business had pivoted to the intersection of art and mysticism, how I'd come to feel that the art-making experience could be a ritual. "We know you can see him here," they told me, referring to Seligmann, and I laughed and winked. It felt really nice to be able to be myself with two people I had just met.

"You must come back," they said. And I did—many times. But let's get back to where this chapter began, six weeks after that initial meeting, when Cody confidently declared that I needed a reading.

"If you think so," I said.

I knew she was right. Every year of my twenties, as I inched closer to my Saturn Return, I had gotten an annual reading from a medium who became a mentor to me. She had since retired, and although we kept in touch, she no longer offered readings so I hadn't had one in a couple years. Considering all of the changes I was experiencing, this seemed like as good a time as any to accept an invitation.

Cody spread out a cloth decorated with a rainbow of zodiac symbols and handed me her deck of cards. After a quick shuffle with a reminder to hold my question in my mind with my eyes closed, she began dealing them out in a spiral. She looked at the cards, made a few comments to me affirming little details and acknowledging minor shifts or adjustments I should make with notes of signs to look out for, then dealt out more cards, continuing the spiral. This repeated until she had dealt out every card from the deck. Then she stopped and looked at me directly for the first time in the reading.

"Why are you worried about everything not working out? You know exactly what you need to do. You're here to help people heal." She pointed at the final two cards: the High Priestess and Temperance. "All you have to do is commit to your spiritual practice. Commit to being the tarot reader you're here to be. Commit to doing the work of healing. Commit to sobriety. As long as you step into this spiritual adviser role and stay sober, everything you were ever worried about will vanish. You know why you're here, and you know what you're here to do. Let all of that other stuff go."

Cody's reading rang in my ears. She was right, of course, but I also knew what *else* it meant. The more clarity I gained from being sober and the more space I had to reflect, the more I was realizing that I didn't want to work in the art world anymore. This truth was terrifying to face because I felt like my whole identity was wrapped up in how I made my living. Even so, it was becoming dissatisfying, more difficult than it was worth. Still, I was afraid—I wasn't sure who I would be if I wasn't curating art exhibitions any longer.

This was the career I had committed to at nineteen, but I just wasn't sure I wanted it anymore. *If I can't find stability through an art career,* I wondered, *then how can I possibly find stability through tarot and witchcraft? In New York City?* That seemed even more impossible and overwhelming. But the reality is that when you change, things change. Your perspective changes, your truth changes, your story changes.

Cody scooped up the cards and placed them back in the box. She folded up the cloth and handed it to me. "I want you to have this. You're going to use it with your clients."

"Oh, I can't," I protested. "That's too much!"

"It's not, and you must," she insisted as she pressed the fabric into my hands.

Her vision was on point, and though I couldn't see it yet, her confidence did provide a spark of hope that perhaps I could figure this out if I followed through on my commitments to a spiritual path and sobriety. I still use that cloth every time I do a reading, laying out the cards on it for my clients.

This spirit of allowing help and guidance from others to open our eyes can be found in the next two cards on the Fool's Journey: Justice and the Hanged Man. Together, these cards reflect the balance of self-examination and surrender that step seven asks for: taking responsibility while also letting go of ego and control. In traditional twelve-step programs, step seven encourages humility through asking our higher power to transform us. In step seven, you take responsibility for your character defects and trust that they can be removed. Like Justice, this step calls for honesty with ourselves and a willingness to accept the results of our past actions while striving for balance and integrity moving forward. Step seven requires recognizing that self-will alone isn't enough and that change comes from a higher power (whatever that means to you). The Hanged Man's lesson of letting go aligns with the idea of surrendering your shortcomings to that power, trusting that transformation will come in time.

JUSTICE

— ◇ —

Accountability, Truth and Clarity,
Consequences and Reflection,
Moral Compass

The Justice card is about themes of balance, fairness, truth, and account-ability. In our context, this card looks at the importance of integrity and fairness in our journey toward sobriety, encouraging a thoughtful and balanced approach to both ourselves and our relationships.

Justice encourages us to take responsibility for our actions. This could mean acknowledging past behaviors and their consequences, which is often a crucial step in the recovery process. Achieving sobriety often requires finding balance in life. The Justice card highlights the impor-tance of balancing emotions, thoughts, and actions, which can help us maintain a healthier lifestyle. This card also squarely values truth. In sobriety, being honest with ourselves and others about struggles, triggers, and progress is vital. This openness can foster stronger support networks and improve our mental well-being. Justice reminds us all that actions have consequences, and reflecting on the impact of substance use on our life and the lives of those around us can reinforce the commitment to sobriety. The card can represent developing a strong moral framework, which can guide decisions and behaviors in sobriety, helping us navigate challenges and stay true to our commitment.

THE HANGED MAN

— ◇ —

*Pause and Reflection, Letting Go and
Surrender, New Perspectives, Sacrifice
and Growth, Patience and Waiting*

The Hanged Man speaks to the themes of reflection, letting go, new perspectives, and the sacrifices necessary for growth—each of which is highly relevant to the journey of sobriety. The Hanged Man often represents a state of suspension, where we are encouraged to take a break or step back from our current situation, surrendering to a higher purpose. In the context of sobriety, we pause to reflect on our habits, choices, and the need for change, and the Hanged Man can signify the necessity of taking time to evaluate our life from a different perspective, which is crucial in the journey toward sobriety, and surrendering the need to control addiction by recognizing that healing often requires accepting help from others, such as support groups or rehabilitation programs.

The Hanged Man is often depicted upside down, illustrating a change in perception. In sobriety we learn to see life without the influence of substances, leading to a clearer understanding of ourselves and our motivations. Sobriety also often requires sacrifice and a willingness to let go of certain friends, environments, or habits that are not conducive to a healthy lifestyle. The Hanged Man can suggest that this sacrifice is necessary for personal growth and achieving a better, more fulfilling life. The card can also speak to the need for patience and the understanding that recovery is a process that may require time and effort. Like the Hanged Man, individuals in recovery may find themselves in a period of waiting before they can fully move forward, and this time should not be wasted.

It can be an opportunity for introspection, learning, and planning for a healthier future.

THE SEVENS OF THE MINOR ARCANA

— ◇ —

The Seven cards of the Minor Arcana are about challenges, introspection, and endurance. They indicate a moment where progress is possible but obstacles must still be overcome, often requiring strategy, inner wisdom, or patience, and they can each reflect the complexities of the journey toward sobriety, highlighting both the challenges and the chances for personal development. Each card encourages us to confront our struggles, make conscious choices, and cultivate resilience in our pursuit of a sober lifestyle.

Seven of Wands

This card often represents challenges and standing your ground. In the context of sobriety, it can point to the struggle to maintain commitment in the face of external pressures or internal fears. It encourages resilience and the importance of defending our choices against opposition.

Seven of Cups

The Seven of Cups speaks to the realm of options, dreams, and illusions. This card can highlight the temptations that come with sobriety—to revert to old behaviors or to escape reality. It prompts reflection on choices and the importance of clarity in decision-making. In sobriety, it can signify the need to choose wisely among various pathways and desires.

Seven of Swords

This card often deals with deception or strategic thinking. In terms of sobriety, it can express the internal struggle with self-deception or avoidance of confronting deeper issues. It might also signal the need for honesty—both with ourselves and with others. This card can remind us to be mindful of self-sabotaging behaviors.

Seven of Pentacles

The Seven of Pentacles is typically about patience, assessment, and long-term growth. This card can relate to sobriety by emphasizing the importance of taking the time to evaluate and invest in personal progress. It signifies that sobriety is a journey that requires nurturing and patience, as well as the understanding that results take time.

—⚬—

Step seven focuses on humility and seeking spiritual improvement by asking a higher power to remove one's character defects. The Justice card emphasizes the importance of personal accountability and the need to confront our past actions and their consequences, which correlates in recovery with the need to recognize and accept our character defects. It encourages us to be fair and open with ourselves, acknowledging where we need change aligned with the spiritual honesty sought in step seven. The Hanged Man takes the process of surrendering to a higher purpose of viewing life from a different angle. In recovery, we need to let go of ego and be willing to allow a higher power to guide our transformation. The Hanged Man teaches that we can grow through surrender, which is central to step seven's focus on humility and the release of character flaws. The Sevens of the Minor Arcana suggest reflection, assessment, and the need for conscious choice.

Together, these tarot cards present a narrative of reflection, accountability, surrender, and growth. They highlight the importance of acknowledging our past and character defects (Justice), the need to let go and embrace change (Hanged Man), and the continued assessment and conscious choice (Sevens) essential for navigating the recovery journey. Each card reinforces the spiritual and emotional work inherent in step seven, showcasing the transformative power of humility and self-awareness in achieving sobriety.

A STEP SEVEN RECOVERY TAROT SPREAD TO SEEK NEW PERSPECTIVE AND EMBRACE HUMILITY

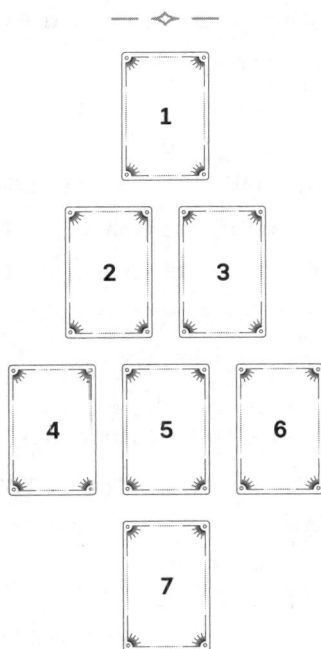

— ✧ —

```
            ┌─────┐
            │  1  │
            └─────┘

      ┌─────┐     ┌─────┐
      │  2  │     │  3  │
      └─────┘     └─────┘

 ┌─────┐  ┌─────┐  ┌─────┐
 │  4  │  │  5  │  │  6  │
 └─────┘  └─────┘  └─────┘

            ┌─────┐
            │  7  │
            └─────┘
```

Step seven calls us into deeper surrender: an invitation to ask our higher power to remove the patterns that no longer serve us. This spread is designed to offer clarity, perspective, and spiritual guidance as you open yourself to transformation through humility. Let each card be a mirror and a message, helping you see the edges of both your strength and your growth with compassion. This is not about perfection; it's about willingness.

Card 1
CURRENT STATE OF MIND

This card represents where you are right now in your recovery journey. It gives insight into how you perceive your shortcomings and your openness to change.

Card 2
STRENGTHS

This card highlights your strengths and positive attributes that can aid you in your recovery process. Acknowledge the qualities you possess that can support your progress.

Card 3
UNDERSTANDING SHORTCOMINGS

This card highlights the specific shortcomings or challenges you face. It may reveal aspects of yourself that you need to acknowledge, let go of, or work on.

Card 4
SPIRITUAL GUIDANCE

This card represents the guidance or support that your higher power is offering you. It's an invitation to listen to messages of love and wisdom regarding your journey.

Card 5
RELEASE AND LET GO

This card illustrates what you need to release in order to move forward. It offers insight into specific fears, habits, or mindsets that are holding you back.

Card 6
ACTION STEPS

This card outlines practical steps you can take to embody humility. It can provide direction on how to integrate your learnings into your daily life with practices, habits, or attitudes to cultivate.

Card 7
OUTCOME

This card represents the potential outcome if you fully embrace this step. It shows what is possible for you in the long run as you work through your shortcomings and embrace humility.

After drawing and interpreting the cards, take time to reflect on how the insights from each card can apply to your life. Consider journaling on your thoughts, feelings, and any actions you plan to take based on the reading. You may also want to meditate on the cards, focusing on how they resonate with you and your journey.

A RITUAL FOR STEP SEVEN: EMBRACING HUMILITY AND LETTING GO

Step seven emphasizes humility and the need to ask for help in letting go of character defects. The idea is that we are encouraged to embrace support and become ready to have our higher power remove our shortcomings.

Materials Needed

Herbs or incense associated
  with purification (my
  preference is rosemary)
  and a means to light this
Two small bowls or
  containers (ideally
  ceramic, glass, or another
  natural material)

Water
Earth (soil/sand)
Piece of paper and pen
Candle (white for purity
  or light blue for clarity)
Feather or leaf

The Spell

+ Find a calm space where you feel connected to nature or your spiritual practice. This could be a serene outdoor space or your Sobriety Altar. Take a moment to ground yourself; breathe deeply and center your thoughts.

+ Light your incense or herbs to create a cleansing atmosphere.

+ Set up your bowls or containers in front of you. Fill one with water and one with earth, symbolizing the cleansing and removal of your shortcomings and the deep-rooted aspects of your character.

+ Spend a few moments in silence, reflecting on your character defects. Think about how they have affected your life and the lives of others. Acknowledge the discomfort they bring and open your heart to the possibility of release.

+ Take your piece of paper and write down the specific character defects you want to release. Be honest and intentional. You might write something like, *I release my fear of failure* or *I let go of my tendency to control.* Fold the piece of paper and hold it in your hands.

+ While focusing on your intention, say a prayer or invoke your higher power by saying out loud: "Great Spirit/Guides/Universe,

I ask for your assistance in letting go of these shortcomings. Help me to embrace humility and grow in my recovery."

+ Place the folded paper into the bowl of water. Visualize your shortcomings dissolving. This symbolizes your willingness to surrender these defects and transform them. Say this affirmation out loud: "I release these burdens to the Universe, allowing them to flow away from me and into the depths."

+ Light the candle, allowing its flame to represent illumination and purity. As you do this, repeat this affirmation: "With your guidance, I embrace humility and release what no longer serves me."

+ Spend a few minutes meditating on the release of those defects. Visualize them dissolving into the water or becoming part of the earth, transformed into something nurturing. See yourself embodying humility, ready to accept help and grow.

+ Take the feather or leaf and hold it in your hands. Speak aloud this affirmation: "With this offering, I embrace the lesson of humility. May I always remember that I am part of something greater and be open to receiving help."

+ When you feel ready, extinguish the candle and express gratitude to the energies, spirits, or higher power you called upon. Take a moment to appreciate the process you've engaged in and the inner work you're committed to.

Over the next few days, reflect on this experience. Consider journaling about any new insights or changes you may notice in your thoughts and behaviors as you embrace your journey in recovery.

DEATH AND TEMPERANCE

✧ ✧ ✧

I AM PATIENT WITH MYSELF AS I INVOKE
MY PERSONAL TRANSFORMATION.

✧ ✧ ✧

"I want you to read cards at the party for my book launch," my friend Vanessa announced on the phone.

I was stunned and immediately felt unworthy of this opportunity. Vanessa is the creator of Chakrubs, the crystal sexual wellness aid that revolutionized both the sex and wellness industries, and she was gearing up to celebrate the release of her new book with a big soiree at the Museum of Sex downtown. I was planning on attending to congratulate my friend, but that was all—I couldn't fathom that she would want me to read cards for the guests at such a major event. I felt sure that there must be others in her network who could do a far better job than I could.

"Wow, I don't know what to say," I stammered.

"Say yes!" she said immediately. "I believe in you; your cards are always on point; and I think you need a little push right now. Be there at 8 p.m. sharp."

And just like that, I was booked for my first event as a tarot reader, and no one had a harder time believing it could be possible than I did.

The lit-up sign of the Museum of Sex flashed as I walked up from the subway. *Here goes,* I thought and walked inside through the gift shop.

"I'm the tarot reader for Vanessa's event?" I said, as if it were a question instead of a statement, to the first employee I encountered.

She directed me downstairs, and I emerged into a beautiful space dimly lit and filled with crystals and candles and stacks of Vanessa's book.

"My love!" Vanessa exclaimed as she threw her arms around me. "I have you all set up right over here. This is going to be wonderful!"

"Will you be my first reading of the night?" I asked her as I settled into my station. "I brought a Crystal Oracle Deck so we can be on theme for you."

Her eyes gleamed. "I would be honored."

We closed our eyes and held hands as I whispered a prayer of intention and protection, like I always did at home before pulling any cards. I gave the cards a quick shuffle and revealed Moonstone, and sharing the reading with her immediately felt natural.

"Your divine feminine energy is right here at the forefront tonight!" I said. "Let it shine! Your intuition led you here; never stop listening to it. This is a transformative night for your personal growth. You are blessed and protected. May all you do this evening come from your heart guided by love, as you always do!"

She took my hand again and said, "That's exactly what I needed to hear. Thank you."

We shared a giggle, and I sat up a little straighter. Maybe I *could* do this. I had to—the event was about to begin. I was going to be brave, face my doubts and insecurities, and do it all sober.

I gave fifty-five readings that night, by far the most I had ever done in one day. A line formed and never stopped as guests took turns sitting with me for a few minutes each. I channeled messages for people feeling doubtful about their love lives, parenting skills, and careers. I cried with a man who was going to be incarcerated in a few days and needed emotional support—his mother came through me with a message of comfort that echoed the one she would share with him in his childhood whenever he was scared. I laughed with another woman whose supposedly commitment-phobic boyfriend was going to propose shortly (he did, and she messaged me a photo of the ring!).

Some of my girlfriends surprised me at the party to cheer me on—the line was so long, I couldn't chat with them until after the party ended when they took me out to the Standard to celebrate with dancing and mocktails. But before we left, I checked my phone to see a text from a friend: *OMG how was the party?? I can't believe you read for Jasmine! She is RAVING about you on Instagram.* I had no idea what or who she was talking about, but when I opened Instagram on my phone, I had over a thousand new followers and 422 unread messages. A striking woman I recognized from earlier in the night had tagged me in a video effusively praising the reading I had given her. Apparently, Jasmine was a model who had became famous on Tumblr due to her innovative style, sharp wit, and effortless cool, and she had turned that notoriety into several lucrative brands before the term *influencer* was even in our lexicon. She was a multihyphenate powerhouse with a record deal, a clothing line, a makeup line, and an outstanding real estate portfolio. And she had shined her light on *me* with a generous shout-out!

Maybe it was time for me to believe in myself as well. That night showed me that sometimes we are our own biggest obstacles and the ones who stand in our own way. It's time to kill that and let it all go, even if it's scary.

At this point in our spin through the Fool's Journey with the cards as our guide, I hope you are feeling more accepting of your sensitive nature and more compassionate toward yourself about where you've been, where you are, and where you have yet to go. As we live a life with more clarity, we gain understanding of why we have the triggers we do, why we respond or react in the ways we do, and how the patterns we've developed as coping mechanisms may not actually help. The stabler we become, the more aware we are and the clearer we see what else needs to end and shift and change.

That's the beautiful, frustrating, and ultimately worthwhile aspect of peeling back the layers: there's always a new layer underneath. We can recognize what we have healed and can put away while noticing what we have yet to deal with. I think it's helpful to remain open to change and growth, new beginnings, and the transformation that comes from endings.

If we think of the path of sobriety as similar to Persephone's ascent from the depths of the Underworld, this is the point in the journey when we emerge and begin to truly recognize our transformation. We are seeing the ways we have harmed others as well as ourselves, and we are restoring balance by transforming our relationships because *we* have inherently transformed. Healing takes time, and there are challenging aspects that we may want to rush through in order to avoid the pain of discomfort. But there's no prize for racing through this and getting to the end.

Step eight in recovery asks us to make a list of all persons we have harmed through our addictions and become willing to make amends to them all. It's crucial to include the ways we have harmed ourselves as well. And this brings us to the next two cards that guide us through the Fool's Journey: Death, the card of transformation and change, and Temperance, the card of balance and moderation.

DEATH

— ◇ —

Transformation, Letting Go, New Beginnings,
Acceptance of Change, Rebirth

The Death card is often misunderstood due to its name. It speaks of transformation, endings, and new beginnings rather than physical death. This card reminds us nothing is ever written in stone—not even a tarot reading, which simply explores one potential future or reality that could come from continuing down our current path.

Sobriety often requires individuals to undergo a significant transformation in their lifestyle, habits, and thought processes. The Death card encourages positive change and the shedding of old patterns, behaviors, relationships, or substances. It marks the end of an old way of life and the liberation that comes with it. And after the ending represented by the Death card, there is always a new phase of life that begins—ideally, since this card is followed by Temperance, a balanced one. In sobriety, this new phase can begin with the opportunity to rebuild our life, establish healthier relationships, and discover new passions.

The Death card teaches acceptance of life's inevitable changes, encouraging us to embrace the journey of recovery as a natural evolution rather than something to be feared. It also suggests the concept of rebirth. Within the context of step eight, Death highlights the importance of letting go of past behaviors and attitudes that contributed to harm in one's life and the lives of others. Embracing the concept of the death of old habits allows us to be ready for the emotional labor of making amends, indicating that past actions need to be acknowledged and laid to rest for the sake of future growth.

TEMPERANCE

— ◇ —

Balance, Moderation,
Healing and Integration, Self-Control
and Patience, Spiritual Growth

The Temperance card is associated with moderation, harmony, and the blending of opposites. (It's also literally connected to the notion of abstaining from substances! Does the temperance movement ring a bell? It was the social and political campaign in the nineteenth and early twentieth centuries that advocated for moderation or total abstinence from alcohol consumption to address perceived social problems and health risks associated with heavy drinking. Temperance advocates believed that restricting or eliminating alcohol use would improve society as well as individuals' lives. We cannot talk about sobriety without the Temperance card!)

Temperance emphasizes the importance of finding balance in life and seeking a harmonious state that avoids extremes, which are crucial for someone striving for sobriety. This card advises moderation in all things, suggesting that instead of completely depriving ourselves, it's about finding a middle ground. It makes me think of how a sober lifestyle is not devoid of fun due to a lack of substance use; it's about cultivating new ways to experience joy and pleasure. Temperance often conveys a sense of healing and integration, so it can also represent the journey of healing from past behaviors and integrating new, healthier habits into one's life. This card encourages self-control and patience, recognizing that the path to sobriety can be a gradual process that takes time and effort. On a spiritual level, Temperance can represent the inner work necessary for transformation, suggesting that sobriety can lead to deeper self-awareness and spiritual growth.

Making amends as part of step eight in recovery is a delicate process that requires careful thought and compassion. This card encourages us to approach our amends with balance and to seek harmony in our relationships, both with ourselves and with those we've harmed. It also blends different aspects of life and reconciliation of past actions with newfound principles, urging us to integrate the lessons learned during recovery into how we handle relationships moving forward.

THE EIGHTS OF THE MINOR ARCANA

— ◇ —

The Eights of the Minor Arcana collectively emphasize themes of change, perseverance, emotional growth, and the effort required to overcome challenges. In the context of sobriety, they highlight both the struggles and the rewards of making meaningful life choices and the ongoing journey of personal transformation.

Eight of Wands
DECISIVE STEPS TOWARD SOBRIETY

The Eight of Wands is about swift movement and progress. So it can point to the rapid changes and developments that can happen once someone decides to embark on a sober journey. It emphasizes the importance of seizing opportunities, being proactive, and maintaining momentum in recovery. This card can also signal the positive energy that can come from an active community or support groups in sobriety. With its connotation of swift action and movement, this card can reflect the urgency and energy needed to take action in making amends. It shows that once the decision is made to restore relationships, the process can progress faster than anticipated, suggesting openness and willingness can lead to positive outcomes.

Eight of Cups
DISTANCE FROM TRIGGERS

This card typically speaks to moving on or leaving something behind in search of deeper fulfillment. It can reflect the emotional journey of recognizing the need for change and leaving behind unhealthy habits or toxic environments and the courage it takes to pursue a life more aligned with our values and well-being. When it comes to step eight in particular, it can represent the willingness to acknowledge those we have harmed and the emotional work needed to confront and make amends to them.

Eight of Swords
WILLINGNESS TO CONFRONT
TRIGGERS AND DIFFICULT EMOTIONS

This card is about feeling trapped or restricted, often by our own thoughts or fears. In the context of sobriety, it may reflect the mental struggles we face when trying to overcome addiction or maintain sobriety. It reminds us that while feelings of entrapment can be overpowering, they are often self-imposed, and liberation is possible by changing our perspective and taking steps toward freedom. Regarding step eight, this card can reflect the feelings of entrapment and mental challenges when thinking about making amends. It emphasizes the need to confront the fears and anxieties arising when we are reaching out to those we've harmed.

Eight of Pentacles
DEVELOP NEW SKILLS WITH
PATIENCE AND PERSISTENCE

The Eight of Pentacles tells us about diligence, craftsmanship, and the pursuit of mastery. Relating this to sobriety, it suggests the hard work and commitment required to maintain a sober lifestyle. Just like skilled craftsmanship, sobriety often involves continuous effort, learning, and self-discipline. This card can represent the journey of building a new life and supporting ourselves through a dedication to personal growth and productivity. In the context of step eight, it suggests that making amends requires effort and commitment. Recovery and mending relationships are not always easy, but the perseverance represented by this card can encourage continued dedication to the process.

Together, Death, Temperance, and the Eights of the Minor Arcana provide a rich tapestry of meaning related to step eight of recovery. They emphasize the importance of transition, balance, hard work, confronting fears, and the willingness to act. Recovery is a journey of personal growth, requiring introspection and the courage to make amends for past harms. Be patient with yourself as you invoke your personal transformation.

A STEP EIGHT TAROT SPREAD TO UNDERSTAND THE HARMS NEEDING AMENDS

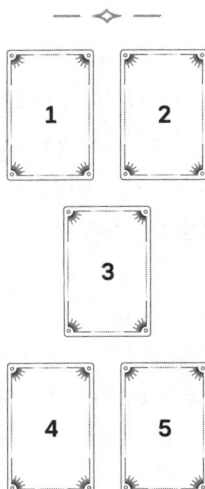

— ◆ —

```
┌─────┐   ┌─────┐
│  1  │   │  2  │
└─────┘   └─────┘

     ┌─────┐
     │  3  │
     └─────┘

┌─────┐   ┌─────┐
│  4  │   │  5  │
└─────┘   └─────┘
```

Step eight is an act of courage and deep honesty: a willingness to face the past and take responsibility for the harm we've caused. This spread is designed to help you reflect with compassion, gain insight into the impact of your actions, and receive guidance on how to move forward with integrity. Let the cards support you in building a foundation for true healing, one rooted in accountability, empathy, and the desire to make things right.

Card 1

THE PAST ACTIONS

This card represents the actions you've taken that may have caused harm to others. It encourages reflection on your behavior and decisions, helping you acknowledge your past.

Card 2

THE IMPACT ON OTHERS

This card sheds light on how your actions have affected the people on your list of those you've harmed. It can reveal the emotional or practical consequences of your behavior on their lives.

Card 3

THE PATH TO AMENDS

This card offers guidance on how to approach the process of making amends. It may suggest strategies, attitudes, or actions to embody as you work toward healing those relationships.

Card 4

WHAT YOU NEED TO LEARN

This card can provide insight into personal lessons that come from this reflection, helping you understand how to grow from your past mistakes.

Card 5

YOUR WILLINGNESS

This card assesses your readiness and willingness to take the steps necessary to make amends. It can reveal any fears or hesitations that may arise.

As you shuffle the cards, focus on your intention to explore your past, understand your impact, and seek guidance on how to make amends. Allow each card's meaning to resonate with your experiences. Write down your thoughts and feelings about each position in the spread. Take the insights gained from the reading and consider how you can apply them to your recovery journey. Make a concrete plan for reaching out to people you wish to make amends with, using what you've learned to guide your approach.

A TAROT SPREAD
FOR UNDERSTANDING
EMOTIONAL SELF-HARM

— ◇ —

This spread can serve as a starting point for deeper self-reflection and healing. Remember to approach this practice with self-compassion and openness, as awareness is the first step toward emotional healing. If you feel overwhelmed, consider seeking support from a mental health professional to help you navigate these feelings.

Card 1
THE SOURCE

This card represents the root of your emotional harm. It can indicate a specific belief, past experience, or behavioral pattern that has contributed to your self-sabotage. This card may uncover underlying reasons or triggers for your self-harming behavior. What beliefs, emotions, or past experiences may have contributed to this pattern?

Card 2
THE BEHAVIOR

This card reflects the specific actions or thoughts you're engaging in that lead to emotional harm. It can reveal self-destructive habits or coping mechanisms that aren't healthy.

Card 3
THE IMPACT

This card speaks to the effects of self-harm on your life. How has this behavior influenced your mental, emotional, or physical well-being? What are the consequences you've faced?

Card 4
THE LESSONS

This card suggests a lesson to learn or a new perspective to adopt that can help you break the cycle of self-harm.

Card 5
THE SOLUTION

This card offers insight into how you can begin healing or breaking free from these harmful patterns. What steps can you take to nurture yourself and promote a healthier mindset?

Before drawing cards, take a moment to reflect on your question and set a clear intention for your reading. As you shuffle, think about your intention and how you would like to understand your patterns and healing. Lay out the five cards in the order depicted on page 141. Take the time to reflect on each card's imagery and meaning, as well as how it relates to your personal situation. After interpreting the cards, make some space for self-reflection. Journaling your thoughts can be especially helpful. Write about the insights you've gained, how they resonate with your experiences, and what actions you might take moving forward.

A TALISMAN FOR COURAGE AND SELF-CONFIDENCE

It isn't easy to admit when we were wrong, face our past mistakes, and make amends, so an energetic reminder of our fortitude can help us confront these challenges. Keep this talisman with you as a symbol of your inner strength and courage whenever you face a challenging situation. My favorite way to make a talisman is through enchanting a sachet of herbs.

Materials Needed

- Incense (my preference is dragon's blood, as it enhances courage) and a means to light it
- Marker
- Sachet bag
- Borage (bravery)
- Thyme (courage)
- Tarragon (empowerment)
- Basil (confidence)
- Rosemary (clarity)
- Yarrow (protections)
- Lemon Balm (calm)
- Other items such as crystals, charms, or coins that speak to your intention (optional)

The Spell

Consider doing the ritual during a moon phase that supports courage, like the waxing moon.

- ✦ Energetically cleanse your space by burning herbs or playing music with a high vibration.
- ✦ Light your incense and invite any supportive elements and guides to come in to support the intentions of your spell.
- ✦ Draw your Sobriety Sigil (see page 19) on the bag with the marker.
- ✦ Fill the bag with your herbs, expressing your gratitude for each one as you do so. You may also wish to add crystals, charms, coins, or anything else to enhance your intention.
- ✦ When the bag is filled, hold it in your hands and close your eyes. Focus on the feeling of courage and say out loud: "I am brave and confident in all situations." Be specific and positive.
- ✦ Spend a few minutes meditating on your intention. Visualize yourself embodying courage and feeling empowered.
- ✦ Pass the talisman through the smoke of the incense, sealing the energy you've infused.
- ✦ Thank any spiritual or natural forces you called upon.
- ✦ Extinguish the incense.

Keep this talisman close. Carry it with you; place it on your altar; or put it in a special place where you can see it daily. Periodically revisit the talisman to recharge its energy, especially if you feel you need an extra boost of courage.

Remember, the power of the talisman comes from your belief and intention. Trust in your ability to harness courage with the help of your enchanted object.

A STEP EIGHT RITUAL TO CULTIVATE WILLINGNESS TO MAKE AMENDS

— ◇ —

This ritual combines reflection, intention-setting, and an opportunity for self-forgiveness to cultivate the willingness to make amends to all of those we have harmed, including ourselves. Keep your Talisman for Courage and Self-Confidence visible and near you while performing this spell.

Materials Needed

Journal or notebook
Pen or pencil

Small bowl or container

The Spell

+ Before you begin, take a few deep breaths to center yourself. Inhale deeply through your nose and exhale slowly through your mouth. Allow any tension to melt away as you focus on this moment.

+ Set your intention by saying this affirmation out loud: "I seek to understand the harm I have caused and to cultivate the willingness to make amends."

+ Take your journal and write down the names of individuals you have harmed, along with the specific actions or behaviors that led to that harm. This could include friends, family, colleagues, or even yourself. Be as honest and detailed as you feel comfortable. Allow yourself to feel any emotions that arise during this process. It's normal to experience sadness, guilt, or regret.

+ Next to each name, write down your feelings about making amends. This part is about acknowledging your feelings and fears without judgment. Ask yourself the following questions:

  * What prevents me from making amends?

* What do I fear will happen?
* How might this person benefit from my amends?

+ After reflecting, take a moment to visualize what it would feel like to make amends to each person. Write a letter to yourself expressing your willingness to make these amends. For example: *I am willing to reach out to [Name] and apologize for [specific actions]. I understand that this may be uncomfortable, but I am committed to my recovery and to healing the relationships I've harmed.*

+ On small pieces of paper, write each of the names of the individuals you've harmed, along with a brief note about the specific harms. As you write each name, hold the paper and acknowledge the pain you may have caused both yourself and the other person.

+ When you are finished, fold the pieces of paper and place them in the bowl or container. This symbolizes your intention to release the burden of these actions.

+ Spend a few moments in silence or prayer, focusing on self-forgiveness. Place a hand on your heart and feel your gratitude for your heartbeat as you say out loud: "I forgive myself for my past actions, and I acknowledge that I am worthy of healing and growth."

+ Close the ritual by thanking yourself for taking this crucial step in your recovery journey. You may choose to keep the pieces of paper in a jar on your Sobriety Altar or dispose of them (you could burn them and dispose of the ashes at the base of your favorite tree or houseplant, for example) as a symbol of letting go.

After the ritual, reflect on your experience and write down in your journal any insights or feelings that emerged. Consider revisiting this exercise periodically as you continue to feel the call to make amends. Remember that recovery is a journey, and cultivating willingness takes time. Engage in open conversations about your experience with a mentor or support group when you feel ready. Be gentle with yourself as you navigate this process.

9

THE DEVIL
AND THE TOWER

✦ ✦ ✦

COMMITTING TO MAKING
MAJOR CHANGES BY RIGHTING
MY WRONGS, I FIND FREEDOM.

✦ ✦ ✦

For many people in recovery, step nine—"Made direct amends to such people wherever possible, except when to do so would injure them or cause harm"—is one of the most intimidating and challenging parts of the twelve steps, so it makes sense that this leg of the Fool's Journey is accompanied by the guidance of two of the most intimidating cards in the deck: the Devil and the Tower.

Let's talk about what making amends is because it's not exactly the same as apologizing. A heartfelt apology is *part* of it, but it's really more about changing the way you move and act with others and setting the intention of reconciliation. It's about accepting responsibility for the wrongs you made in the past and actively working on improving your behavior and the relationship (if that part is possible—it may be that you don't have a relationship anymore, and if that's what's right for the other person, you need to work on accepting that because part of this step is acknowledging when you *can't* make amends without causing further harm). A crucial aspect is to fix the initial problem you caused—again, only if that is possible.

Not everyone is going to be pleased to see you pop up in their lives again, and some people may not want to hear from you at all. We must be ready to handle the consequences of our past actions. Just because you want to move on doesn't mean they do, too. It's ultimately their decision whether to engage with you, hear you out, or grant forgiveness. Making amends is only for situations that won't have a negative impact or cause additional harm to any parties involved, which also includes *you*. You do not need to reopen painful memories by reconnecting with anyone who has caused you immense emotional distress—you could always choose to acknowledge your part in the matter through ritual without initiating contact with them—and you *certainly* do not need to reach out to anyone who abused you. That wouldn't be productive for your own self-love or self-care, and those are also crucial elements of this part of sobriety.

Ultimately, amends are doing whatever we can to make things right as best we can. Active addiction is inherently self-centered, so this is your opportunity to instigate real changes, think about what you're doing before you do it, and take others' feelings into consideration before acting on impulse or solely in your own interests.

Together, the next cards in our journey—the Tower and the Devil— reflect the destruction of old, harmful patterns and the courage to break free, leading to the healing transformation of step nine's willingness to face the consequences of past actions.

The Tower represents sudden upheaval, the collapse of illusions, and the breaking down of false structures. In step nine, making amends can feel like a Tower moment—terrifying, humbling, and disruptive. It can shake up relationships, force painful truths into the open, and dismantle old defenses. But just like the upheaval of the Tower ultimately clears the way for growth, step nine leads to freedom and spiritual renewal. The Devil symbolizes bondage, addiction, and self-imposed limitations. Before recovery, many people are trapped in destructive cycles of behavior, much like the figures chained to the Devil's throne. Step nine helps break these chains by taking responsibility for past wrongs. However, the Devil also warns of the temptation to avoid this step—whether through denial, shame, or rationalization. Facing the Devil means confronting the ego and fears that resist change.

THE DEVIL

— ◇ —

Addiction and Temptation, Confrontation
with Shadows, Materialism and Distraction,
Feeling Trapped, the Path to Liberation,
Reflection and Responsibility

The Devil card represents themes of temptation, addiction, materialism, and entrapment. Its imagery speaks to bondage and self-imposed limitations. Before recovery, many people are trapped in destructive cycles of behavior, much like the figures chained to the Devil's throne. The Devil can also signify being tied to material possessions or distractions that prevent personal growth. And even though this card serves as a potent reminder of the struggles of addiction, I believe that means it can also strongly support the journey toward sobriety. It emphasizes the need for self-awareness, commitment to confront inner challenges, and ultimately the potential for liberation and growth. The Devil card also suggests the allure of addiction and how it holds us back from experiencing true freedom. This card encourages us to confront our inner demons and the underlying issues that may contribute to addiction. It teaches that acknowledging these aspects is a crucial step toward recovery.

The Devil also warns of the temptation to avoid step nine—whether through denial, shame, or rationalization. Recognizing these feelings can motivate us to seek liberation. Facing the Devil means confronting the ego and fears that resist change. And step nine helps break these chains by taking responsibility for past wrongs. While the card highlights darkness and challenge, it also reminds us of the possibility of breaking free. By making amends, individuals begin to release themselves from the guilt and shame associated with their addiction, breaking the chains that bind them to their past mistakes.

Sobriety often involves a journey of self-discovery, healing, and empowerment. The Devil card prompts self-reflection, encouraging us to take responsibility for our choices.

THE TOWER

— ◇ —

*Breaking Down Old Structures, Awakening,
Crisis and Opportunity, Release from
Illusions, Embracing Change*

The Tower shows a moment when the foundations of a person's life are shaken, leading to necessary transformations and a reevaluation of beliefs and patterns. In the context of sobriety, the Tower card can act as a catalyst for profound change, urging us to confront our challenges head-on and to rebuild our lives on a stabler and more authentic foundation. The Tower can signify a powerful moment of awakening or realization—which might be the moment of clarity when someone recognizes the need for change, prompting them to seek help or make a commitment to sobriety. Sobriety often requires dismantling old habits and patterns of behavior. The Tower represents the breaking down of those structures that may have supported unhealthy coping mechanisms, making way for new, healthier choices by righting our wrongs.

While the Tower's chaotic imagery of lightning strikes and people leaping from windows can be intense and appear frightening, it also presents an opportunity for growth. In the journey toward sobriety, the chaos and disruption that may accompany making a transition can ultimately lead to the freedom of a healthier, more authentic life. The Tower often symbolizes the shattering of illusions or false beliefs, like the false comforts that substances can provide. It encourages embracing change and being open to the transformative process, even when it feels difficult or painful. Making amends allows us to clear the debris from our past and lay a new foundation for healthier relationships moving forward.

THE NINES OF THE MINOR ARCANA

— ◇ —

The Nines of the Minor Arcana highlight different aspects of personal struggle and success. In the context of sobriety, they underscore the importance of resilience, emotional fulfillment, self-reflection, and the rewards that come from hard work and dedication. The Nines suggest a culmination of experiences and a step closer to personal growth through introspection, fulfillment, and nearing completion of a cycle. We are almost there—but not quite yet—and the Nines acknowledge this tension.

Nine of Wands
KEEP GOING DESPITE SETBACKS

This card often symbolizes resilience, perseverance, and trials to be faced. In the context of sobriety, it can represent the struggles and battles we must endure while overcoming addiction. It encourages us to stay strong and committed to our recovery journey, reminding us that

we are close to overcoming our challenges, even if we feel worn down. In recovery, step nine requires the tenacity to face one's past, communicate honestly, and work toward mending relationships despite previous challenges.

Nine of Cups
PRIORITIZE EMOTIONAL WELL-BEING AND FIND JOY IN LIFE WITHOUT SUBSTANCES

Often referred to as the "wish card," the Nine of Cups signifies emotional satisfaction and the fulfillment that comes with achieving personal goals, including those related to recovery. It suggests that through sobriety, we can attain true happiness, as well as the manifestation of wishes that might have seemed out of reach during times of addiction. In step nine, the journey to making amends can lead to a sense of achievement and joy, as we reconnect with others and heal relationships, ultimately bringing emotional peace.

Nine of Swords
ADDRESS YOUR ANXIETIES TO FIND PEACE AND CLARITY

This card indicates anxiety, fear, mental anguish, and sleepless nights. In the context of sobriety, it can reflect the emotional challenges and fears that may arise during recovery. It reminds us that confronting our anxieties is a part of the healing process and it's important to seek support and address these feelings instead of letting them overwhelm us. It can speak to the guilt and remorse that might accompany reflecting on past wrongs. Acknowledging these feelings can be crucial in the amends process.

Nine of Pentacles

CULTIVATE A SENSE OF
STABILITY AND SECURITY

Symbolizing self-sufficiency, independence, and achievement, the Nine of Pentacles shows us the rewards of hard work and personal effort. This card emphasizes the value of self-care and the importance of building a life that reflects our values and goals. It suggests that through dedication to sobriety, we can cultivate a sense of autonomy and enjoy the fruits of our labor. In terms of step nine, this card tells us that through making amends, we not only mend emotional relationships but also contribute positively to our own stability and self-worth, fostering a sense of pride in our progress.

Taken together, the Devil, the Tower, and the Nines of the Minor Arcana highlight the struggles of addiction but also the potential for transformation through the processes of acknowledging past harms and making amends. Engaging with their symbols can offer a deeper understanding of the emotional and spiritual journey of recovery as we work through our past by making amends to build toward a better future.

A TAROT SPREAD TO CULTIVATE DISCIPLINE AND TAKE RESPONSIBILITY

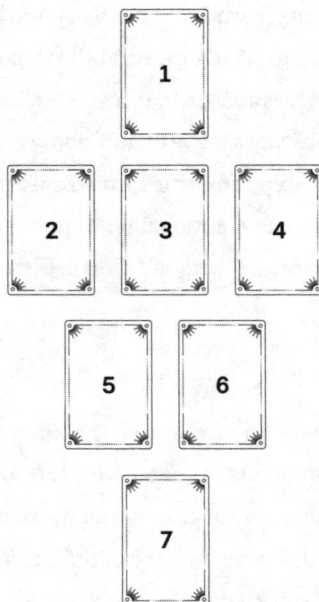

— ◇ —

```
        ┌─────┐
        │  1  │
        └─────┘

┌─────┐ ┌─────┐ ┌─────┐
│  2  │ │  3  │ │  4  │
└─────┘ └─────┘ └─────┘

   ┌─────┐ ┌─────┐
   │  5  │ │  6  │
   └─────┘ └─────┘

        ┌─────┐
        │  7  │
        └─────┘
```

A tarot spread focused on understanding and embodying step nine can offer insights into your feelings and motivations and how to approach making amends.

Card 1
CURRENT STATE OF MIND

This card represents your present emotional or mental state regarding your journey in recovery and the process of making amends.

Card 2
OBSTACLES TO MAKING AMENDS

This card highlights any fears, doubts, or beliefs that may be holding you back from taking the necessary steps for amends.

Card 3
LESSONS FROM THE PAST

This card provides insight into what you've learned from past mistakes and how those lessons can inform your approach to making amends.

Card 4
THE IMPORTANCE OF FORGIVENESS

This card reveals how forgiveness of yourself and others plays a role in your process of making amends and in your overall recovery.

Card 5
ACTION STEPS

This card suggests concrete actions you can take in making amends and embodying the spirit of this step.

Card 6
SUPPORT AND GUIDANCE

This card indicates what or who might be supportive in your process of making amends, whether that's a person, a community, or even a personal strength.

Card 7
OUTCOME OF MAKING AMENDS

This card offers insight into the potential outcomes of your journey in making amends and how it can positively impact your life.

Approach the reading with an open heart and mind! Take a moment to meditate on each card and its meaning. Consider how it relates to your understanding of step nine. Write down your thoughts and feelings about each card. How does it resonate with your personal experience in recovery? Based on the cards, what specific actions can you take? Consider discussing your insights with a sponsor, therapist, or trusted friend who understands the recovery process. Think about how you can embody the messages from your spread in your daily life moving forward.

A RITUAL FOR MAKING AMENDS

This ritual can serve as a powerful personal tool to deepen your understanding of step nine, focus your intentions on healing, and bring a sense of spiritual support to the making of amends.

Materials Needed

Two candles (one white and one blue) and a means to light them
Paper and a pen or pencil (optional)

A crystal (such as rose quartz for compassion or clear quartz for clarity)

The Spell

+ Begin by taking a few deep breaths to center yourself. You might want to visualize roots extending from your body into the earth, grounding you.
+ Arrange your materials on your Sobriety Altar. Light the white candle, symbolizing purity, healing, and the intention of making

amends. Light the blue candle, representing peace, forgiveness, and understanding.

+ Call upon your higher power and any supportive energies that resonate with you. Say this affirmation out loud: "I invite the energies of healing and forgiveness to guide this process as I seek to make amends."

+ Spend time reflecting on the people you have harmed and the pain caused by your actions. Write letters to these individuals if you feel it is appropriate. Express your remorse, acknowledge the harm done, and state your intention to make amends. You don't have to send these letters unless you feel ready. It is the intention and acknowledgment that are most important. (You may wish to revisit any notes you made in your journal after your Step Eight Spell; see page 145.)

+ Hold your insights in your mind or your letters in your hands and focus on the energy of regret and healing. Say out loud: "I am committed to living a life of integrity, honesty, and love. I seek to mend the past and create a better future."

+ Hold your crystal in your hand and close your eyes. Visualize the positive changes you wish to embody and the amends you plan to make. Imagine sending love and healing toward those you have harmed.

+ Meditate on your commitment to changing behaviors and taking responsibility.

+ You can perform a symbolic act of release, such as burning the letters in a firesafe container to transform those feelings into healing energy or burying them in the earth as a way to honor the past and plant seeds for new growth. Close the ritual by thanking your higher power and any energies who came through to support this spell and extinguishing your candles.

Spend time after the ritual reflecting on your emotions and intentions. Journal about your experience and any insights you gained. Consider how you can begin to take actionable steps toward making amends in your daily life. Write down specific things you commit to, whether it's reaching out to someone to have a conversation or taking a larger step toward restitution. As a gesture of goodwill and reconciliation, consider making a small offering to the earth or the energies invoked. This could be flowers, seeds, or something meaningful that symbolizes your desire to heal relationships. You could also make a charitable donation (even something small is good!) to a foundation that supports recovery, animals, the Earth, or something else meaningful to you.

Be open to opportunities to make amends in real life, remembering that the process may take time. Celebrate small victories on your path to healing.

10

THE STAR
AND THE MOON

✧ ✧ ✧

A DEEP COMMITMENT TO SELF-REFLECTION AND HONESTY ALLOWS ME TO SEE MY WRONGS AND PROMPTLY RIGHT THEM.

✧ ✧ ✧

As the months of not drinking flew by, I was getting more comfortable in new social situations, but crowds, large gatherings, and meeting a lot of people at once still made me uneasy. So when I was asked to join a coven, my initial reaction was: *No, not for me!* Of course, I had friends who were witches, but we didn't do rituals together. Spiritually, I was a lone wolf, even though my Sobriety Altar featured a circle of witches.

So what was I doing manifesting this and then turning it down? Why was I saying no? Did I feel unworthy, not knowledgeable enough in the occult, not cool enough for this? Was I expecting to get rejected before I even tried? Sometimes when we are presented with something we think we want, we don't feel ready for it. But I realized I had done too much work to run away, and sobriety had taught me to honestly consider what would be the worst that could happen if I went. And beyond that, what if it turned out to be better than I could even imagine? When a friend who had also been invited texted me to ask if I was going, I agreed to try it out with her. We both felt a little apprehensive, but we decided it would be better together and we could always leave if it didn't feel right. Sobriety has taught me we don't have to do difficult things alone, and there's often help if we seek it!

We shared a ride to the coven meeting, and our car pulled up to a beautiful old brick apartment building with an arched doorway, somewhere on the border of Bed-Stuy and Bushwick in Brooklyn.

"No turning back now," I said, grabbing my friend's hand and leading the way to the front door. "Let's go!"

We buzzed in and made our way up the winding staircase in the marble foyer, following the muffled sounds of excited conversation and laughter emanating from a door slightly ajar. I tentatively pushed it all the way open and was immediately greeted by a small, fluffy black cat who tilted her head to gaze at us before swiftly turning around and slinking down the long hallway. We followed the cat to a lush living room dimly lit with candles bright enough to reveal a small group of people lounging on velvet couches around a coffee table filled with fruit and bread and cheese.

"Hello!" "Welcome!" "We were wondering when you two would arrive!" "We are so excited you both are joining us!" We received such a warm welcome as everyone stood up to hug and greet us. I recognized a few of the faces: the friend who had invited us, a woman I had met on Instagram through our shared interests in art and witchcraft, an artist whose work I had followed online. I immediately realized there was nothing to feel intimidated by here.

My experiences that night taught me I'd been wrong when I'd made assumptions around what being in a group of fellow witches could feel like and encompass. One aspect of recovery and sobriety I love is the lesson that it's OK to make mistakes and we can change our perspectives through humility. With self-reflection we can admit when we were wrong and open our hearts and minds to be receptive to constructive criticism. Even our basic mindset can change when we take our pride and ego out of the equation!

If I had operated on my previous assumption that I didn't need to be a part of a coven or a witch community (even though deep down within myself, I *did* desire that sort of connection), I would have missed out on so many beautiful opportunities, wisdom, and friendships that have come through this shared experience. Step ten states that we "Continued to take personal inventory, and when we were wrong, promptly admitted it," and this experience reminds me that honest self-assessment and admitting when we could be wrong in our actions or our mindsets while embracing our community lead to our spiritual growth. I know it has led to mine.

Community is a crucial part of recovery because being a part of something bigger than you is grounding and offers greater perspective. Whether or not you want to join a coven, I think it's important to create new community connections by leaning into a cause that means something to you and getting involved in it. Whether you feel passionately about animal rescue, prison reform, mental health care access, supporting those who have survived domestic violence, or even particular aspects of recovery such as harm reduction and education, find a group that works in your local community and *get involved!* Volunteer your time, attend meetings, assist in fundraising, do whatever you can to support the cause. I promise you'll be shocked at how healing it can be.

If you *do* want to join a coven, my advice is to use your resources! Look for Pagan, Wiccan, or witchcraft groups in your area. Online options like Meetup, Facebook groups, and other social media communities, or even the bulletin board in a local coffee shop can be good resources. Visit metaphysical shops or spiritual bookstores; they often have community boards with listings of groups and events. Participate in open rituals, workshops, or festivals related to witchcraft and paganism. This will allow you to meet others in the community and get a feel for different practices. Some covens and groups may also have their own online presence, so you can reach out directly.

You can even take the initiative yourself—it's not as intimidating as it sounds! You might already know more witches than you realize. Practices like manifestation and astrology have entered the pop culture lexicon in a major way, and *everyone* is familiar with the moon, so it could be easier to start your own coven than you ever dreamed. You can help your friends recognize their magic by inviting everyone over for snacks and intention-setting on an evening that just so happens to fall on the night of the full moon!

When you do find potential groups, be open about your intentions and what you are looking for in a coven. It's important that their values and practices align with your own. Take your time to find a group that feels right for you. Trust your intuition about the people and the environment. Joining a coven is often a commitment, so find a group with which you feel comfortable. Witchcraft is so self-empowering on its own, especially for those who have been othered, but we do still need one another. And being a part of community is an essential aspect of maintaining our sobriety, too. I truly believe that once we set an intention, the Universe always assists us in making it true. Remember, my coven found *me* and yours will find you, too, even if you have to create it to make it so.

It feels rather appropriate that the next two cards in the Fool's Journey are the Star and the Moon as we explore the idea of magical communities and covens—we witches love the celestial beings of the cosmos, and we can all benefit from their guidance!

THE STAR
— ◇ —

Renewal and Healing, Hope and Inspiration,
Connection to Your True Self, Spiritual Guidance,
Balance and Harmony, Vision for the Future

The Star card is a symbol of hope, inspiration, and renewal. Its imagery typically features a figure pouring water, representing the flow of emotions and the balance between the conscious and unconscious mind. Its themes can be particularly relevant to sobriety and recovery as it signifies a period of healing and regeneration, often after a time of confusion. The Star serves as a reminder of the light that exists even in darkness, encouraging us to look forward to a brighter future. Change is possible, and a fulfilling life beyond addiction is achievable. This card also encourages us to reconnect with our innermost desires and values. Sobriety often involves rediscovering our authentic self free from the influences of substances. Many people in recovery also find strength and guidance in spiritual practices like those associated with the Star.

In sobriety, finding balance—another of the Star's themes—between emotions, relationships, and self-care is crucial for maintaining a healthy lifestyle. The Star invites us to dream and set goals. Our ongoing personal inventory at this stage in step ten encourages reflection and self-assessment, both of which can lead to deeper insights and healing. The Star emphasizes the importance of hope and positivity in recovery, suggesting that by acknowledging and addressing our shortcomings, we become more attuned to inner guidance and potential for growth.

THE MOON

— ◇ —

Illusion and Deception, Intuition and
Inner Guidance, Facing Fears, the
Subconscious, Cycles and Patience

The Moon is a card of illusions, intuitions, the subconscious, and the duality of human nature. When it comes to sobriety, its themes are both a warning about the seductive nature of substances and a guide toward deeper understanding and healing. It emphasizes the importance of awareness, confrontation of fears, and reliance on inner wisdom during the journey of recovery.

The Moon card can represent confusion and uncertainty: it cautions not to be swayed by distorted perceptions. Instead, the Moon encourages introspection and tapping into our intuition. For someone in recovery, this can be a powerful tool. Reflecting on our feelings and thoughts can help us understand our triggers and the deeper reasons behind substance use. The Moon often brings up fears and anxieties we need to confront, and this is something those of us on a sobriety journey must face head-on. This card indicates many issues related to addiction can stem from the subconscious mind, suggesting that therapy, journaling, or other forms of self-exploration may be beneficial. The Moon is inherently also linked to cycles and phases—much like the path of recovery, which requires patience and acceptance of its natural ups and downs.

The Moon reminds us to confront not only our conscious thoughts but also the deeper, perhaps hidden emotions and fears that can surface during self-reflection. Step ten calls for honesty in our ongoing self-inventory, which includes addressing our illusions or misconceptions about ourselves. With this card we see we can trust our intuition while navigating this path—acknowledging that some truths may be uncomfortable but are essential for continued growth.

The traditional step ten involves carrying on taking a daily personal inventory and promptly admitting when we are wrong. On its face it's a continuation of step four's fearless moral inventory, but it's not about continuing to beat ourselves up about when we are "wrong." It's about self-reflection, honesty, and maintaining spiritual and emotional balance. The Star symbolizes hope, guidance, clarity, and healing. Step ten speaks to faith in a higher power, renewal, and the promise of a better path the Star shows us. Recovery allows us to deeply commit to ourselves—to the serenity and clarity that come with consistent honesty with ourselves. By maintaining a spiritual connection and staying accountable, we align ourselves with the hopeful, healing energy of the Star. The Moon, on the other hand, reminds us that not everything is as it seems, and it challenges us to face our inner doubts and hidden truths. This mirrors step ten's warning to be vigilant about self-deception and denial. The Moon cautions that without honest reflection, we may fall back into old patterns of fear or confusion.

Together, these cards illustrate the balance in step ten: the Moon calls us to look at our flaws and fears honestly, while the Star reassures us that healing and progress are always possible through continued self-awareness and spiritual connection.

THE TENS OF THE MINOR ARCANA

— ◇ —

The Tens of the Minor Arcana represent different aspects of completion, culmination, and transition. For a sobriety journey they offer insights as they depict progression toward resolution and fulfillment. They emphasize the duality of challenges and serve as guides illustrating the potential outcomes of maintaining sobriety and the realizations that come from overcoming struggles.

Ten of Wands
THE HEAVY WEIGHT OF
ADDICTION AND RECOVERY

This card represents burdens and responsibilities. It often conveys feeling overwhelmed. In the context of sobriety, the Ten of Wands could indicate the heavy load of addiction or the struggle to maintain balance while navigating recovery. However, it also highlights the importance of seeking help and support to relieve these burdens. Addressing our responsibilities and learning to set them down can be an important part of the sober journey.

Ten of Cups
JOY COMES FROM
LIVING AUTHENTICALLY
WITHOUT SUBSTANCES

This card shows us emotional fulfillment, happiness, and harmonious relationships. In the context of sobriety, the Ten of Cups can represent the joy and contentment that often come from being sober, as well as the positive relationships that can be nurtured and deepened when we are clearheaded and present. The ultimate emotional rewards of a sober lifestyle include its healthy connections with family and friends.

Ten of Swords
THE WORST IS OVER

This card represents the darker aspects of struggle—betrayal, loss, or a painful ending—but also the potential for transformation. In relation to sobriety, it can reflect the pain and the "rock bottom" moments many of us face before seeking recovery. It may suggest the end of a harmful cycle and the recognition that we must let go of old patterns to move forward.

Ten of Pentacles
THE LEGACY OF HEALING

Associated with material success and legacy, the Ten of Pentacles reflects stability and long-term achievement. It may highlight the importance of building a solid foundation for the future in recovery. This card underscores the benefits of sobriety in terms of financial stability and creating a reputation that makes our loved ones proud. It suggests sobriety contributes to a healthier, securer environment for ourselves and our family.

＿＞˙○˙＜＿

Step ten involves a continuing personal inventory and prompt admission of any wrongs. It encourages us to maintain an ongoing awareness of our thoughts, actions, and feelings for emotional and spiritual growth. When we examine this concept against the Star, the Moon, and the Tens of the Minor Arcana, we can further understand the nuances of self-reflection and accountability that help maintain sobriety as we begin to put this new way of life into practice.

By integrating the meanings of the Star, the Moon, and the Tens of the Minor Arcana into the framework of step ten in sobriety, we can find encouragement and guidance in our recovery journey. These cards remind us to remain hopeful, confront fears, nurture our emotional and relational wellness with a deep commitment to ourselves, and understand that the path to healing can involve both completion of old struggles and laying the groundwork for a healthy future. Through continuous self-reflection and accountability, recovery becomes a transformative journey toward a brighter, more hopeful existence.

A TAROT SPREAD
TO MAINTAIN
SELF-AWARENESS

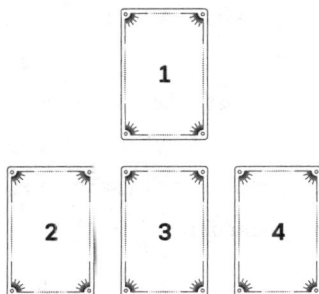

— ✧ —

```
        ┌───────┐
        │   1   │
        └───────┘
┌───────┐┌───────┐┌───────┐
│   2   ││   3   ││   4   │
└───────┘└───────┘└───────┘
```

Step ten of recovery tells us to continue taking personal inventory and promptly admitting when we're wrong. This tarot spread can help you understand and embody this step by focusing your attention on self-reflection, pathways for growth, and accountability, fostering a deeper awareness of yourself and your interactions with others as you continue to maintain your sobriety.

Card 1
CURRENT SELF-REFLECTION

To understand where you currently stand in your sobriety and in your self-reflection process.

This card represents your current feelings, thoughts, and behaviors regarding your sobriety journey.

Card 2
WHAT NEEDS
ACKNOWLEDGMENT

To identify any recent wrongs or mistakes that need to be addressed.

This card focuses on situations or interactions from the recent past you may need to confront or apologize for as part of maintaining accountability in your life.

Card 3
GUIDANCE

To provide insight on how to approach personal responsibility.

This card offers guidance on the best way to address your wrongs and suggests a course of action. It may indicate what you should communicate or how you should approach a situation or something that could benefit from acknowledgment or revision.

Card 4
STEPS FOR CONTINUED GROWTH

To outline ways to continue your personal inventory and growth.

This card suggests practices, attitudes, or mindsets that will support your ongoing journey and aid you in developing further self-awareness.

As you shuffle the cards, contemplate step ten and your journey in sobriety. Focus on each card's meaning as you draw them. Take time to interpret each card individually and then consider how they relate to each other. Reflect on the messages they convey and journal about your interpretations, insights, and feelings about them. Based on your insights, consider what specific actions you can take in the coming days or weeks to embody step ten in your sobriety.

This tarot spread can be a supportive tool in your recovery process. Remember that the cards offer guidance and reflection but, ultimately, the power lies in your willingness to engage with them and take meaningful steps in your journey.

A TAROT SPREAD FOR CHANGING YOUR MIND

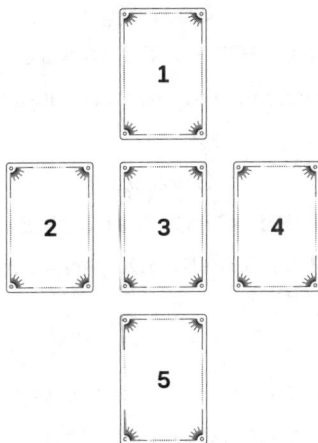

Sometimes the most powerful magic is giving yourself permission to shift. This spread is here to help you explore your current mindset, uncover hidden influences, and open the door to new perspectives. Whether you're feeling stuck, uncertain, or simply ready to see things differently, these cards offer a path to clarity, expansion, and conscious change.

Card 1
CURRENT MINDSET

What is my current perspective or belief about the situation?

Card 2
UNDERLYING INFLUENCES

What underlying factors or emotions are influencing my current mindset?

Card 3
ALTERNATIVE PERSPECTIVES

What are some different viewpoints or options I haven't considered?

Card 4
ADVICE FOR CHANGE

What attitude or action should I adopt to facilitate a change in mindset?

Card 5
POTENTIAL OUTCOME

What might happen if I embrace this new perspective?

Before you shuffle the deck, take a few moments to focus on what you want to change your mind about and why. Take deep breaths to center yourself. As you shuffle your cards, think about your intention. When you feel ready, draw five cards for your spread. Lay the cards in order and begin interpreting them based on their positions, pulling in traditional meanings with your own intuitive guidance. Once you have interpreted the cards, take some time to reflect on what each card means for your situation. Journaling your thoughts can provide further insight and clarity in the present moment or to come back to later.

A TAROT SPREAD FOR COMMUNITY CONNECTION

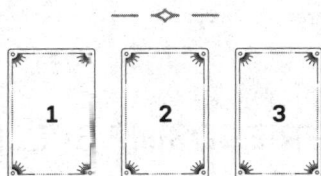

—— ◇ ——

```
┌─────┐  ┌─────┐  ┌─────┐
│     │  │     │  │     │
│  1  │  │  2  │  │  3  │
│     │  │     │  │     │
└─────┘  └─────┘  └─────┘
```

Connection is essential to both healing and growth. This spread is designed to help you reflect on your current relationship with your community, recognize the gifts you bring, and uncover new ways to engage more meaningfully. Whether you're seeking belonging, service, or deeper roots, let this reading guide you toward more aligned and heart-centered connection.

Card 1

YOUR CURRENT RELATIONSHIP WITH YOUR COMMUNITY

This card represents your feelings, thoughts, and connections to your community at this time. It provides insight into any barriers or strengths in your existing relationships or involvement.

Card 2
WHAT YOU CAN OFFER
TO THE COMMUNITY

This card reflects what skills, talents, or resources you can share with your community. It helps you understand how you can contribute positively and make meaningful connections.

Card 3
OPPORTUNITIES FOR
DEEPER CONNECTION

This card indicates potential opportunities, events, or experiences that might help you deepen your connection with your community. It can offer guidance on where to focus your energy or attention.

A FRIENDSHIP SPELL
— ◇ —

Through the clarity of sobriety, we unearth our core personal values and gain a greater understanding of what we need from others. As you grow, new aspects of yourself need to be fed and nurtured, and you may discover new things you enjoy. While this can open up new dimensions in your existing friendships, it can often mean making new friends as well who share these interests. This is my spell for calling in new friends. It is best performed on a new moon.

Materials Needed

Incense or herbs for
cleansing (optional)
Candle (pink for friendship)
and a means to light it
A carving tool (optional)

Piece of paper and pen
A small offering to nature like
seeds or flowers (optional)

The Spell

+ Prepare your space by cleansing the energy. Light your herbs and gently waft the smoke around your space. As you do this, visualize it clearing away any negative energy and creating a welcoming atmosphere. Before moving further into the ritual, you may wish to carve your intentions into the candle, which could include the word *friendship* or any symbols that connote this desire.

+ When you are ready, light the candle while focusing on your desire to forge new friendships.

+ Take a few deep breaths and allow your thoughts to settle. Take the piece of paper and write down what qualities you seek in new friends. Be specific but open to possibilities. For instance, you might write *I wish to find friends who share my desire for sobriety* or *I seek friends who are kind and supportive of sobriety* or whatever feels aligned with your desires when it comes to friendship.

+ Close your eyes and visualize yourself surrounded by new friends, sharing laughter and joy. Picture the connections you hope to make and the experiences you wish to share with your new friends.

+ If you have a small offering for your deity, higher power, or nature itself, place it near your altar as a thank-you for bringing new friendships into your life. (Pink roses, a symbol of friendship and love, would be my suggestion.)

+ When you feel ready, close the ritual by expressing gratitude for the energy and intentions shared. You can also say aloud a simple affirmation like, "I am open to new friendships and connections." Extinguish the candle and keep the paper with your intentions in a place where you'll see it often, like on your altar or in a journal.

And now this is the extra magical part: after your ritual, take proactive steps to meet new people. Join groups or clubs that align with your interests, attend local events, or participate in community activities. Keep your heart open to new experiences and don't hesitate to reach out to those you meet!

A SPELL TO FIND YOUR COVEN

— ◇ —

To best prepare for this ritual, take time to reflect on what you seek in a coven. Consider qualities you value (trust, support, shared beliefs) and what you wish to learn or experience (rituals, community, shared goals). Let this intention guide you through this spell.

Materials Needed

Incense (like sage or lavender)

Candle (preferably green for growth or white for clarity) and a means to light it

Carving tool (optional)

Piece of paper and pen

Small cauldron or firesafe bowl

Herbs or crystals that resonate with your intention (such as rosemary for connection, mint for friendship, or chamomile for harmony and citrine for abundance, rose quartz to open your heart to others, or labradorite to enhance psychic connections)

Representations of the four elements (earth, air, fire, and water) to bring balance and invite support (this could include a bowl of salt or soil, a feather, a candle, and a small dish of water)

Other personal items that hold significance (optional)

The Spell

✦ Begin by lighting the incense. (Choose one that feels calming and connective, like lavender or sage.) Allow its smoke to gently cleanse your space, signaling to the Universe (and yourself) that you are ready to call in sacred connection.

✦ Create a sacred space at your altar by casting a circle. You can do this by walking in a clockwise direction around your area, visualizing a protective boundary of light.

✦ Call upon the elements and any deities or spirits you work with, inviting them to join you in your intention.

✦ Take a few moments to ground yourself. Focus on your breath; feel the earth beneath you; and visualize roots extending from your body into the ground, anchoring you.

✦ You may wish to carve your candle with your intention to connect with a coven, using symbols for this desire, the word *COVEN*, or any combination that feels best for you.

✦ Place the candle in front of you and light it as a symbol of bringing clarity and illumination to your search for community.

✦ Take the piece of paper and write down your intention for finding a coven. Be specific about what you hope to gain and contribute. An example would be, *I seek a supportive community that shares my passion for nature and magic.*

✦ Place the written intention in the cauldron or bowl. Add a pinch of the herbs or a crystal as an offering to the spirit of community. As you do this, visualize your intention manifesting and the connections you wish to create with your future coven.

✦ Close your eyes and visualize yourself surrounded by magical like-minded individuals. See yourself participating in rituals, sharing knowledge, and feeling a sense of belonging and support. Feel the energy of the group and allow this to resonate within you. Stay in this moment as long as you wish.

✦ When your spell is complete, thank the Universe, the elements, and any deities for their guidance and support. Acknowledge the energy you have raised and trust that your intention will be heard. Close your circle by thanking the elements and any beings you invited in. Imagine the boundary dissolving and grounding yourself back in the present moment.

As you move forward, stay open to opportunities and connections that may arise. Notice any signs or synchronicities that may arise. Attend local events, workshops, or gatherings to meet others who share your interests. Look for online communities, social media groups, or local events where you can connect with potential coven members. Building relationships takes time, so be patient and authentic in your search. Trust that the Universe will guide you to the right people for your coven as you allow your personal journey to unfold naturally by remaining open to the signs and chances that come your way.

A RITUAL
TO CONNECT
WITH COMMUNITY

— ◇ —

Recovery teaches us that we don't heal in isolation, we heal in connection. And yet opening ourselves up to community can be one of the most tender and vulnerable parts of the journey. This ritual is meant to honor that. It's a way to intentionally call in connection, support, and shared energy— to move beyond fear or loneliness and into the sacred space of being seen, held, and mirrored by others.

This isn't about perfection or performance. It's about gathering in authenticity, in softness, and in shared intention. Whether you're calling in a new circle, deepening the relationships already in your life, or simply reminding yourself that you *are* part of something larger, this ritual creates space to anchor that truth.

Let this be a ceremony of belonging—one you craft with care, with courage, and with the quiet knowing that you're not meant to walk this path alone.

Materials Needed

Candles (I recommend a mix of pink for friendship, blue for clear communication, white for new beginnings, and yellow for positivity) and a means to light them

Bowl of water (for reflection)

Small dish of salt (for purification)

Incense (optional, for creating a sacred space and enhancing connection. My preference for this spell would be sandalwood or palo santo.)

Natural items (stones, leaves, flowers) to represent community

Paper and pen

Preparation

My preference is to perform this spell on the full moon, but you should choose a date that holds significance for you—you might choose the new moon, equinox, or solstice, when energy is heightened. Once you have chosen the date, it's time to pick your location! Select a serene spot in nature where you feel connected and comfortable. Don't overthink it or make it too complicated. My favorite place for rituals is near the ocean, but since I live in Manhattan, I often utilize the park in my neighborhood. You could perform this ritual alone, but at this moment in your sobriety journey and considering the intention of this spell, I think this is a wonderful opportunity to invite others who are interested in finding community as well. Ask everyone to bring a natural element that holds meaning for them: a shell, a favorite flower, a feather, etc., as well as a snack to share with the group.

The Spell

+ Clear the area of any debris and feel the ground beneath you. Arrange the candles safely in a circle to establish a physical representation of community. Place the bowl of water and dish of salt at the center for reflection and purification. Light the incense if you are using it, setting the intention for the space.

+ Set up a space designated for snacks and drinks if you choose to have them, such as a table or picnic blanket. After everyone is welcomed and sitting in a circle, invite your guests to place their natural elements and talismans within the circle with the candles and other items.

+ Stand or sit comfortably; close your eyes; and take several deep breaths. Lead the group in visualizing roots extending from their feet into the earth, connecting with the vast community of living beings around you.

+ Call in the four cardinal directions (East, South, West, North) and the elements (Air, Fire, Water, Earth) to witness your ritual and lend their energies.

+ Invite everyone to write down their intentions for this ritual: *I seek community*, or something specific that resonates with each individual. As you write, think about the qualities and values you seek in a community: support, friendship, shared interests, etc.

+ Instruct everyone to take a moment to sit quietly with the bowl of water, reflecting on their intentions while visualizing the type of community each desires. Imagine meeting individuals who share your values and passions. Exchange warmth, laughter, and ideas.

+ Invite everyone to go around the circle to share their intentions for community as well as explain the natural element they brought with them and why.

✦ You may say a few words of gratitude to the Universe for the connections you'll make, affirming your openness to new individuals and experiences. Thank any deities, spirits, or elements you invited into your space as well as everyone for coming and sharing their intentions for community connection. Open the circle by respectfully bidding the quarters farewell. Blow out the candles, visualizing your intention being released into the Universe.

✦ Continue to exchange experiences, thoughts, or feelings from the ritual over the shared snacks. When it's time to depart, clean up together to leave the space better than you found it! And so it is!

11

THE SUN AND JUDGEMENT

◇ ◇ ◇

MY HIGHER PURPOSE PROVIDES A GUIDING LIGHT ON MY DIVINE PATH.

◇ ◇ ◇

When you are healing and growing, shifting and transforming, there are few greater signs in a tarot reading to affirm your hard work than the appearance of the Sun. As you overcome obstacles, the Sun shines her beautiful rays of warmth, positivity, and loving guidance to illuminate happiness, joy, and contentment, reminding us there is always a bright side to any situation.

One of the sunniest parts of my practice is meditation, which has become a favorite social activity. It's so funny to think about how a solo spiritual exercise came to replace going out to bars and getting drunk for me, but a good guided meditation that unlocks the imagination has the transcendent power to become truly psychedelic. We don't actually need substances to expand our minds; that's just the pathway we already know. Sobriety affords us the opportunity to develop other tools that are far more beneficial.

With the clarity and confidence I found through my commitment to continued sobriety, my tarot business was steadily taking off, and it became necessary for me to seek out a dedicated space to see my clients in person. I'd been conducting readings in Central Park or in my apartment or running all over the city to the clients' homes, but it was time to feel a little more grounded and professional. The perfect opportunity came when my friend Anka mentioned at dinner one night that she and her business partner were wondering if I'd be interested in a space within their newly expanded tattoo studio in Brooklyn. It still felt uncomfortable to ask loved ones for any help as I was navigating how to ask for what I wanted directly, so this offer really touched me. I could feel tears in my eyes as everything began to fall into place to facilitate my growth.

The studio soon became a second home as I saw my clients sporadically throughout the week and every Sunday, which became Anka's and my day together with our clients. We would always stay after work those Sundays to participate in whatever esoteric workshop was happening, but the one that had the most profound impact on me was a Higher Self Guided Meditation facilitated by a woman named Dyanna who soon became a friend, too.

We all gathered in a circle, and Dyanna led us through a guided meditation to meet our higher self. Your higher self refers to an enlightened, wise, or divine aspect of your consciousness. It's the part of you that is connected to a greater spiritual awareness, inner wisdom, or universal truth. Essentially, this is the best, most authentic version of you—beyond ego, fear, and limitations—offering wisdom and guidance when you tune in to it. I had never even tried to contact whoever mine could be, but I was excited to find out what this being might look like. Everything felt so spacious and thrilling and unexpected, like a very important guest was about to arrive. I set the intention to be open to the experience as we moved deeper into an altered state of relaxation through deep breathing and Dyanna's prompts.

Surprisingly, I found myself on the runway of a deserted airport. A sleek white airplane landed on the tarmac, bringing fluffy white clouds down to earth with it, and a stairway was wheeled up to welcome the passenger. As the door opened, the scene shifted to the look of fuzzed-out Technicolor film and the whole environment began to sparkle. A figure emerged, smiling and wearing a floor-length, iridescent white caftan. Her pastel pink hair was parted down the middle and cascaded in waves that bounced as she slowly descended the stairs. As I looked closer, I realized it was me—but a version of me that I didn't know could exist.

She radiated a softness, quiet confidence, and compassion through her eyes and her smile. My energy seemed like such a contrast to hers—I felt frantic: not as chaotic as I used to be but definitely not chill or as fully present as I wanted. It seemed like I was always anxiously thinking of the next move with wild impatience. There was something so soothing about her presence. She walked over to me and stared with a warm loving gaze for a moment before she spoke: "Hello, my darling. It's me, I'm you, and we are together. Everything will be OK because it always is." She gave me a long hug, smelling of vanilla and roses and sandalwood. And in that moment, I felt that everything would be OK.

After the meditation ended, we went around the circle and each participant shared who they met as their higher self. Others described a savage beast, a feral creature, an animal-human hybrid—there was a running theme of wildness in the room. I felt markedly different, but it was the first time in a long time that I felt like different could be OK because sobriety was making me sit a little better in my own skin. Instead of shying away from sharing out of fear, I spoke up proudly when it was my turn.

"I met myself," I said. "Well, a different version of myself. She was so calm and warm and loving and self-assured. And she sparkled. Everything sparkled! It was wonderful. I didn't even know that version of me could exist."

A small part of me wished I had seen something more fantastical like the others, a wild creature. But our higher selves aren't something we need to or should control. We see what we *need* to see, and I didn't need a wild beast. When I was drinking and getting high, I'd been something of a wild beast. What I really needed instead was a gentle, loving guide to reassure me I could be the person I wanted to be, so that's who came through for me that day.

The more I healed, the more I softened because I finally felt safe to do so. I was able to act out of love and not fear. As the months and years passed, my outward physical appearance began to shift and transform to match the higher self I had envisioned without much conscious thought on my part. Slowly, I let go of what I now see was a protective, harsh look I had cloaked myself in: saturated cerulean hair with jagged bangs, sharp black cat eye makeup with crimson lipstick, and an all-black clothing uniform. Black, the protective color of boundaries, no longer felt comfortable and slowly was replaced by lighter shades of cream and white. I grew out the jagged bangs, and my hair took on a softer, rosier hue that I wear in soft waves. Without even thinking about it, in a few years I came to look like my higher self, and my energy has evolved to match hers as well. I still have my frantic days and my freak-outs, but sobriety helps me remember to stay calm, get grounded, and just breathe my way through it.

Step eleven, which says we "Sought through prayer and meditation to improve our conscious contact with the Universe, praying only for knowledge and understanding of our own highest will, the Divine plan and the power to carry that out," focuses on seeking spiritual growth and connection. This step encourages individuals to improve their conscious contact with a higher power, seeking knowledge of that power's will for them and the strength to carry it out. And the tarot cards that accompany this step—the Sun, Judgement, and the Pages and Knights of the Minor Arcana—represent tools for that effort. Together, these cards underscore the importance of actively engaging in a spiritual journey and finding the guiding light on our divine path.

THE SUN

— ◇ —

Clarity and Enlightenment, Joy and Vitality, Growth and Success, Community and Connection, Warmth and Positivity

The Sun card is typically associated with positivity, joy, success, and enlightenment—a powerful symbol of the potential rewards and positive transformations that come with sobriety, encouraging us to seek clarity, joy, and connection. The Sun also represents truth and the shedding of darkness. For those of us pursuing sobriety, this can speak to the clarity of mind and spirit that comes from being sober, as well as the enlightenment that we gain when confronting personal challenges and struggles with addiction. Sobriety can lead to a more vibrant life, filled with genuine joy and emotional stability, and the Sun encourages us to embrace those pleasures in a healthy and fulfilling way.

The Sun also represents the personal growth and milestones achieved on the journey toward recovery. It reminds us that perseverance leads to a brighter future. The imagery of the Sun card often includes children, bringing their innocence and connection to our attention. Building healthy relationships and finding connection in community can be essential parts of a sober life. This card embodies the joy that can come from achieving a deeper connection with oneself and a higher power in step eleven. It announces the clarity and optimism experienced when we move forward in our recovery, embracing life with renewed energy and understanding.

JUDGEMENT

— ◇ —

Self-Reflection, An Awakening,
Forgiveness and Release, Transformation,
Accountability, New Beginnings

The Judgement card encourages us to assess our past actions and make decisions that lead to personal growth and positive change. It expresses how introspection opens the potential for a more fulfilling life. Judgement prompts a thorough evaluation of our choices and behaviors, as well as their consequences. Through that accountability we can awaken to a higher purpose. In the context of sobriety, this can signal the moment when an individual realizes the need for change—recognizing the desire to move beyond addiction and toward a healthier life.

But Judgement isn't only about more fearless self-exploration; it also speaks to themes of forgiveness, both of ourselves and others. In recovery, letting go of guilt or shame related to past behavior is crucial for healing and moving forward. And in Judgement we find a period of transformation and renewal. It extends the warming rays of the Sun into a guiding light on our divine path. Sobriety is inherently a process of transformation, as we strive to rebuild our lives, relationships, and sense of self without the influence of substances. Judgement trumpets the dawn of a new chapter.

Step eleven suggests that through prayer and meditation, we can gain insights into our past behavior, recognize the lessons learned, and embrace a transformative journey toward spiritual awakening. Judgement encourages us to release old patterns and step into a renewed self—one more aligned with our higher purpose and values.

THE PAGES AND KNIGHTS
OF THE MINOR ARCANA

— ◇ —

The Pages and Knights of the Minor Arcana can carry significant meanings related to the themes of sobriety and personal growth. Pages are harbingers of the potential for new beginnings and the importance of learning and growing, while Knights emphasize the active pursuit of goals and the necessity of courage in overcoming obstacles. Together, they encourage a balance of self-exploration and determined action—a foundation for a successful journey toward sobriety and personal transformation.

The Pages
INNOCENCE AND NEW BEGINNINGS,
CURIOSITY AND EXPLORATION,
AWARENESS AND GROWTH

The Pages are often seen as messengers, heralding new beginnings, learning, and the exploration of emotions and ideas. They open the door to a fresh start and encourage exploration of our feelings and motivations. The Pages can also usher in a period of growth and self-discovery.

The Page of any suit can be seen as embodying the spirit of exploration of step eleven. They express openness to the process of prayer and meditation, a willingness to learn and gain insights into our spiritual existence, and the determination to cultivate a deeper understanding of ourselves and our higher power.

Knights
COURAGE AND COMMITMENT,
CHALLENGES AND CONFLICTS

Knights are all about action, movement, and determination. They embody the pursuit of goals and ideals. They signal the determination needed to maintain sobriety—facing challenges head-on and demonstrating resilience. Knights can also represent the struggles we face on the path to sobriety, helping us prepare and strengthen our resolve.

The Knights also symbolize the commitment to put spiritual principles into action within step eleven of the recovery process. They support us in finding the courage to seek a deeper connection through dedicated practice and to actively pursue knowledge and understanding.

<hr />

WANDS (PASSION, CREATIVITY, ACTION): Staying sober requires motivation to make lifestyle changes. The dynamic energy of Wands inspires embarking on new adventures and projects without reliance on substances.

PAGE OF WANDS: This Page brings in enthusiasm and inspiration and encourages a fresh start and the exploration of creative avenues. In the context of sobriety, it can symbolize starting new projects and pursuing passions without dependence on substances.

KNIGHT OF WANDS: This Knight is often rushing toward goals, representing action and adventure. In sobriety, this card speaks to the drive to pursue life with fervor, seeking excitement and fulfillment in a sober lifestyle.

<hr />

CUPS (EMOTIONS, RELATIONSHIPS, INTUITION): Sobriety often involves recognizing and processing our emotions without substances. Pages and Knights in this suit guide individuals to embrace their feelings in a healthier way.

PAGE OF CUPS: This Page announces new emotional experiences and creativity. In sobriety, this could symbolize the exploration of new emotional depths, healing old wounds, and expressing feelings authentically.

KNIGHT OF CUPS: Often seen as romantic or idealistic, the Knight may represent the pursuit of emotional fulfillment in healthier ways. This card reflects the journey toward emotional balance and sincerity in relationships.

⁓⁓ ⚬ ⁓⁓

SWORDS (THOUGHTS, COMMUNICATIONS, CHALLENGES): Clear thinking and communication are crucial for recovery. Utilizing the analytical aspects of Swords helps to address underlying thoughts, fears, and challenges of sobriety.

PAGE OF SWORDS: This Page heralds curiosity and clarity of thought. This card might suggest the importance of straightforward communication and honest self-reflection in sobriety, addressing mental challenges as they arise.

KNIGHT OF SWORDS: Often portrayed as assertive and driven, this Knight can speak to the determination to overcome obstacles and battles associated with addiction, encouraging swift action toward mental clarity and decisiveness.

⁓⁓ ⚬ ⁓⁓

PENTACLES (MATERIAL ASPECTS, WORK, HEALTH): Building a stable life post-addiction often involves focusing on our health, career, and financial responsibilities. The Pentacles encourage practical steps and commitments toward a sustainable sober life.

PAGE OF PENTACLES: The Page expresses a desire for knowledge and practicality in new beginnings. This card can signal focusing on personal development, skills enhancement, and laying down a stable foundation for a sober life.

KNIGHT OF PENTACLES: The diligent and responsible Knight of Pentacles embodies the steady and methodical approach toward building a sober and secure life, focusing on work and practical matters over impulsive behavior.

A TAROT SPREAD
TO GET TO KNOW YOUR
HIGHER SELF

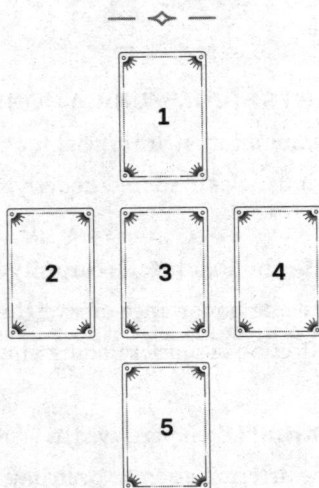

— ◇ —

```
          ┌─────┐
          │  1  │
          └─────┘
┌─────┐  ┌─────┐  ┌─────┐
│  2  │  │  3  │  │  4  │
└─────┘  └─────┘  └─────┘
          ┌─────┐
          │  5  │
          └─────┘
```

Step eleven focuses on seeking to improve our conscious contact with a higher power through prayer and meditation. This step emphasizes the importance of spiritual growth and maintaining a connection to something larger than we are. Use this spread to initiate a meeting with your own higher self!

Card 1
CURRENT SELF

This card represents your current state, mindset, or situation in life. It reflects where you are right now on your journey. It may offer insights into how you feel about your connection to a higher power or the spiritual aspects of your recovery.

Card 2

OBSTACLES TO
SPIRITUAL CONNECTION

This card reveals any fears, doubts, or limiting beliefs that may be hindering your connection with your higher self.

Card 3

GUIDANCE

This card offers wisdom or advice from your higher self regarding your personal growth and spiritual path.

Card 4

KEYS TO FACILITATE YOUR RELATIONSHIP
AND STRENGTHENING CONNECTION

This card represents your innate strengths or abilities you can harness to better connect with your higher self. It suggests practices, rituals, or mindsets to deepen your spiritual practice. It may highlight new ways to engage with prayer, meditation, or self-reflection.

Card 5

FUTURE CONNECTION

This card envisions your spiritual path moving forward. It signifies the potential outcomes or transformations as you continue to seek a deeper connection and understanding of your higher self in your recovery journey.

Take a few deep breaths and set an intention for connecting with your higher self with an open mind and open heart. While shuffling the cards, think about your desire to understand and connect with your higher self. Draw the cards and form a cross with one card at the top, three cards across, and one card at the bottom (see page 190). Spend time with each card as you reflect on its symbolism, imagery, and how it relates to its position in the spread. Write down your thoughts and feelings about each card and how they speak to your understanding of your higher self. After you've interpreted all the cards, take a moment to reflect on the overall message and what actions you might take to foster a deeper connection with your higher self. Consider meditative practices, mindfulness, or any steps (including the spell in this chapter!) that resonate with you that can enhance your spiritual journey. As you navigate step eleven, remember that every person's spiritual journey is unique!

HIGHER SELF
CHECK-IN SPREAD

— ◇ —

After meeting your higher self, this spread can be used to continue to develop your relationship. It's a lovely way to have a quick and easy check-in for guidance and reflection through the wisdom they offer you! This spread can be used regularly to track your growth and development in connecting with your higher self as you continue your spiritual journey.

Card 1
CURRENT STATE
*What Is My Current Connection
to My Higher Power?*

This card represents your current relationship with your higher power or your spiritual self. It may reveal feelings of distance, connection, doubt, or faith.

Card 2
GUIDANCE
What Can Enhance
My Spiritual Practice?

This card offers advice on how you can enhance your spiritual practice, whether through meditation, mindfulness, or prayer.

Card 3
ACTION
What Action Can I Take
to Deepen My Contact with My
Higher Power/Higher Self?

This card suggests a specific action or mindset you should adopt to strengthen your conscious connection with your higher power.

A RITUAL TO MEET AND BECOME YOUR HIGHER SELF

— ◇ —

Step eleven emphasizes the importance of spiritual growth, connection, and seeking guidance, and a beautiful way to embody these principles is through a ritual to meet your higher self.

Who is your higher self? What do they look like? How do they respond? What are their values? How do they conduct themselves? What do they smell like? How do they spend their free time? How do they have fun? What music do they listen to? What are they wearing on a Friday night, a Sunday afternoon, or a Tuesday? Consider every aspect of this version of you because you get to decide who you are now and moving forward into the future!

Materials Needed

Herbal tea or water
Journal and a pen or pencil
Sheet of cardstock or
   other durable paper
Glue

Magazines, collected
   images, photos
Scissors
Glitter, paint, markers,
   crayons, colored
   pencils, stickers

The Spell

+ Create a sacred space where you can be undisturbed. Cleanse the area with incense, tidy up, and put on music that makes you feel good. Arrange your altar or workspace with your materials.

+ Set your intentions by saying out loud "I set this space to connect with my higher self, to understand my path and embrace my truth."

+ Take a few deep breaths, inhaling through your nose and exhaling through your mouth. Close your eyes and focus on your breath while allowing thoughts to come and go without attachment. Visualize a light surrounding you, growing brighter with each breath, connecting you with your higher self. Imagine this light filling you with divine wisdom and insight. Invite in your higher self to join you.

+ After your meditation, open your eyes and take a few moments to gather your thoughts. Write down in your journal any insights, feelings, or messages that came through during your meditation or that you feel connected to in this moment. Consider questions like: What does my higher self want to tell me? or How can I align more closely with my true path?

+ Once you finish writing, take a sip of your herbal tea or water. As you drink, visualize it nourishing your body, mind, and spirit, enhancing your ability to receive guidance.

+ Create a portrait of your higher self using your materials. Do not limit yourself! Include as many aspects of who your higher self is as you can, including words, affirmations, and pictures.

+ When your artwork is complete, close the ritual by thanking any energies, deities, or spirits (including your higher self) you may have called upon during the ritual. Take a moment to visualize sealing the insights you've gained, carrying them with you.

+ Take a photo of your artwork and make it the background photo on your cell phone for eleven days. Place the original on your Sobriety Altar.

Over the next few days, reflect on your experience and the insights that came through from this ritual. Consider incorporating a daily meditation or prayer focused on your higher self into your routine to continue this journey.

12

THE WORLD

✦ ◇ ✦

MY JOURNEY OF SPIRITUAL AWAKENING IS NEVER
COMPLETE BECAUSE THERE IS ALWAYS MORE
TO DISCOVER THROUGH THE LESSONS OF
PRACTICING SOBER MAGIC IN ALL MY ENDEAVORS.

✦ ◇ ✦

Here we are at the end of the journey! We have made it to the World card
and the final step of the process. But is it really over? Of course not—it
never is! And that's something wonderful. Sobriety provides us a new lease
on life and the ability to change and transform over and over again.

Because of the beautiful commitment we have made to clarity, to
understanding ourselves better, and to doing our best with the resources
we have cultivated, we now have opportunities that could not have been
possible before—or at least would not have been sustainable in the long
term. Now we can create our own blessings, and we can receive them more
easily without getting in our own way because we recognize our patterns
and triggers and know how to deal with them. We can feel our feelings and
acknowledge our fears without letting them consume us. We get to *live life
fully present.*

I believe that one of the greatest aspects of step twelve—"Having had a spiritual awakening as a result of these steps, we tried to carry this message to others and to practice these principles in all of our affairs"—is that all you have to do now is put the lessons you are learning into practice: all you need to do is be yourself. This is such a radical act! Just by believing in yourself, being yourself, you become an inspiration for change, an example of the power of transformation. You show the world that a sober life doesn't mean becoming a hermit who gives up everything fun or pleasurable: it means becoming more capable and present in order to truly enjoy everything life has to offer. It means creating the changes you wish to invoke by showing up more fully in every aspect of life.

We all tell ourselves stories—good, bad, and every shade in between—but sobriety empowers us to *change* our story and write a new one. The past decade of my life looks nothing like what I expected it to, and it's honestly far better. This Fool's Journey has taught me that everyone longs to feel loved and accepted and "normal," whatever that may be, and as soon as we love and accept ourselves, the challenges of life become far easier.

And people will be able to tell just by looking at you. There are so many benefits to sobriety—and I am not going to lie to you, the vanity aspect is one of them! It feels *good* when people notice how good you look! Your skin becomes clearer and the color returns; you gain the confidence and self-assurance to dress the way you really want; you are more aware of the choices you make so you become healthier. You value yourself more, so you put more effort into yourself because you know you are worthy of it. But the true radiance comes from within: feeling good makes you look good, too.

And you never know who you could be inspiring simply by existing in this way! By the end of my first year of sobriety, I felt more aligned with my truest self. I was teaching workshops about color magic and sex magic and got cast on a TV show to share these modalities. I was giving tarot readings I was truly proud of with new levels of insight. I had deepened my connections with the most important people in my life—because getting sober doesn't mean you have to say goodbye to everything from your old life; you can fortify any semblance of light that's there—and I'd made new friends, too. And I was having *fun*, more fun than I had ever had before. Through the steps, I learned that I could conquer my fear of not being the "fun one" anymore. When that was my superlative, I wasn't actually having that much fun anyway, so why did I need to hold on to it?

A fellow party girl from my past reached out to me as I neared my first year of sobriety to share that she thought she had a problem with alcohol and needed to stop, but she didn't know how to exist without her defining story of being the wildest one at the party. "I don't know anyone who looks to be having more fun than you," she said. "Can you help me?" I was honored she confided in me, and I couldn't believe she still thought I was fun. We went to a recovery meeting together shortly after, and we still meet up regularly to catch up over seltzers.

Before I posted about my one-year sober anniversary on social media, a friend warned me doing that could kill my career and I should reconsider sharing that part of myself so publicly. It reminded me of what people in the art world had told me years earlier about publicly proclaiming that I was a witch in an interview for an international magazine. Neither killed my career: both of these identities actually made it stronger.

I understand that this is an immense privilege, as not everyone is in a position to be themselves out loud so fully, about their sobriety or their witchcraft. For those people, I want to be one of the examples of what being yourself can look like, even if that means allowing myself to be vulnerable and sharing my struggles. We all have them, so I figure let's not pretend that we don't. And the notion of sobriety, what it looks like and what it encompasses, has changed dramatically in recent years as people make a collective effort to center mental health and well-being. I like to think that as a society, we are shifting to a more accepting reality of the notion that we all need help and it's OK to ask for it.

When I blacked out from excessive psychic energy at my friend's show after many attempts at not just getting sober but *staying* sober and finally with several years under my belt, it was the first time it really hit me how vastly different my life had become now that I was no longer blacking out regularly and being self-destructive. It made me wonder, what was different about this time that I finally did it?

Was it because the depth of my rock bottom was so bad? It can *always* be worse. Was it my circumstances? Maybe. My willingness? Definitely. But the biggest difference this time around that has allowed me to maintain continuous sobriety for this long, is my devotion to my spiritual practice. The support I have found through tarot and witchcraft saved my life. These spiritual tools provided me with a greater understanding of myself, a deeper connection to the Universe, and a new career path that feels meaningful and satisfying. My life truly began once I got sober, and if you feel like yours is waiting to begin, there's no better time than now to start your own Fool's Journey through sobriety with the assistance of tarot, ritual, and witchcraft. Thank you for reading and for letting me be of service.

We have reached the end of this book's Fool's Journey with the World, but our journey is never truly over. One of the joys of this life of ours is that we cycle through many journeys over the course of our days. The World card shows us what to wrap up for this cycle before we get to begin again.

THE WORLD

— ◇ —

*Completion of a Cycle,
Integration and Balance, Success and
Fulfillment, Connection and Unity,
Invitation for New Beginnings*

The final card of tarot's Major Arcana announces completion, fulfillment, and the realization of our goals. It tells us of a sense of wholeness and harmony, often suggesting that a journey has come to a successful conclusion. The World card can be a powerful symbol of the journey toward sobriety and the rewards that come with it, encapsulating themes of both balance and new beginnings.

The World marks the end of a significant phase or journey. In the context of sobriety, this can be an individual who has reached a point of stability and achievement in their sobriety. The card often showcases a sense of balance and integration of different aspects of life, and achieving sobriety can lead to a more harmonious existence, where we learn to integrate our past experiences with our current lifestyle, promoting emotional and mental well-being. Achieving sobriety can bring about a deep sense of pride and success from overcoming significant challenges and now living a life aligned with our true selves. This card also suggests a sense of interconnectedness with the world around us. In sobriety, we often seek new connections and healthier relationships, embracing community and support systems that contribute to our overall wellbeing. And although it represents completion, the World also signals the beginning of a new chapter. For those of us in sobriety, this can mean opportunities and possibilities that lie ahead, encouraging us to embrace new experiences and paths.

The energy of the World aligns with step twelve, which advises, "Having had a spiritual awakening as a result of these steps, we tried to carry this message to alcoholics and to practice these principles in all our affairs." The World is the culmination of a journey and the achievement of a long-sought goal. Completing the twelve steps is just such a journey taking us to a state of understanding and healing akin to the sense of wholeness of the World. Step twelve also emphasizes carrying the message of recovery to others, fostering a sense of community and connection. The traditional imagery of the World card is a dancer stepping into the circle of life—making that connection with a greater whole and sharing the lessons of this journey's end. In step twelve, we acknowledge a spiritual awakening of personal growth and the realization of a higher purpose that often comes with sustained sobriety. Overall, the World encapsulates the journey toward wholeness, community, and the ongoing commitment to help others of step twelve. Now that we are ready to share our experience, strength, and hope with others—helping them on their own journeys toward recovery—we are setting out on a new path with even more to discover.

THE QUEENS AND KINGS OF THE MINOR ARCANA

— ◇ —

*Be of Service, Empathy and Connection,
Leadership and Inspiration*

The Queens and Kings of the Minor Arcana show us different facets of personal strength, emotional intelligence, rationality, and practical skills. Each card encourages an approach that integrates inner strength, emotional health, logical reasoning, and practical life management, all vital components to maintaining a sober lifestyle and achieving personal growth.

The Queens of tarot have gained wisdom through experience and matured to master and creatively utilize their power within a specific element or area of life with a deep connection to intuition and emotional intelligence. The Kings of tarot focus more on outward control through their area of mastery, aiming to have a larger impact for the greater good of the world. Each card encourages the act of service in a unique way, whether it's offering emotional support, sharing wisdom, or providing practical resources. Both Kings and Queens inspire those around them, demonstrating the power of leadership in personal recovery journeys.

The Queens and Kings make me think of what it feels like to truly have some time under your belt in sobriety: the calm, steadiness, and capability achieved through cultivating the tools taught by the twelve steps. Step twelve is about reaching a place of spiritual awakening, where the lessons of recovery are not only internalized but also shared with others. It marks a point of integration—where sobriety is no longer just about personal healing but also about service, community, and giving back. The Queens and Kings show us how to embody these lessons and inspire others.

***

QUEEN OF WANDS: This Queen's confidence, charisma, and inspiration can be harnessed in recovery to encourage others and lead by example. The Queen of Wands embodies a passionate approach to service, motivating others to find their inner strength. She shares the energy to pursue passions, connect with others positively, and take assertive actions to achieve personal goals.

KING OF WANDS: A natural leader who inspires others through vision, creativity, and courage, the King of Wands encourages outreach and the sharing of our journey to serve as a beacon of hope for those still struggling. This King suggests taking charge of our life and decisions to pursue our dreams with determination.

***

QUEEN OF CUPS: This Queen signals emotional intelligence, compassion, and nurturing and emphasizes the importance of empathy in recovery. By connecting emotionally with others, we can offer the heartfelt support and understanding essential for healing. As a guide in sobriety, the Queen of Cups encourages self-care and emotional healing.

KING OF CUPS: This King announces emotional stability and the ability to compassionately guide others through difficult times.

The King of Cups speaks to the importance of maintaining emotional balance while helping others navigate their recovery in step twelve. In sobriety, he aids in fostering healthy emotional expression and resilience.

꒰ ⁘ ꒱

QUEEN OF SWORDS: The Queen of clarity, truth, and insight, this card encourages setting boundaries, honesty, and clear communication when helping others to ensure our message is straightforward and rooted in personal experience. The Queen of Swords urges a rational approach to problems, which is vital in addressing triggers and challenges in recovery.

KING OF SWORDS: A symbol of authority, fairness, intellect, and strategic thinking, this King shares the importance of using wisdom and discernment in recovery work, serving as a guide for others while maintaining our own boundaries. As a sober guide, he encourages the use of logic and ethics in decision-making.

꒰ ⁘ ꒱

QUEEN OF PENTACLES: This Queen expresses practicality, nurturing, and a grounded approach to life. She highlights the value of providing tangible support, whether that's resources, time, or understanding, to those in need of help. In sobriety, she points to the importance of creating a stable environment and focusing on long-term financial and practical goals.

KING OF PENTACLES: The King of stability, security, and the ability to provide for others, he shares the importance of creating a solid foundation for ourselves and others in recovery, offering practical wisdom. He tells that hard work and responsible planning are essential for maintaining financial stability and personal well-being in sobriety.

A TAROT SPREAD TO BE OF SERVICE

— ◇ —

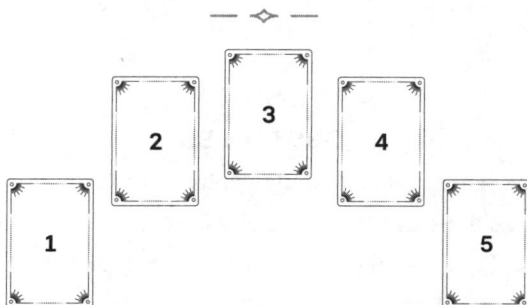

Step twelve involves sharing our experiences to help others and support their journeys. This spread explores the inner journey and the outward expression of recovery through service.

Card 1

SELF-REFLECTION

What do I need to understand about my own recovery?

This card represents your current state regarding your recovery journey. It highlights areas of growth, lessons learned, and aspects you may still need to work on.

Card 2

SHARING EXPERIENCE

What experiences should I share with others?

This card suggests specific experiences or lessons that are vital for you to communicate. It will show how these experiences can resonate with others and provide insight or support.

Card 3

HOW TO HELP

What is the best way for me to help others in their recovery?

This card reveals strategies or methods you can employ to effectively assist others. It may pertain to your strengths, skills, or resources you can utilize.

Card 4
OBSTACLES

What challenges might I face while helping others?

Here, you'll discover potential obstacles or fears that could hinder your ability to be there for others. This card can point to internal doubts or external circumstances to be mindful of.

Card 5
OUTCOME OF SERVICE

What is the potential outcome of my service to others?

This final card provides insight into the impact your efforts may have on both yourself and those you are helping. It gives a glimpse of the rewards of service, such as growth, connection, or healing.

Once you lay out the cards, take time to contemplate the messages each one brings. Record your thoughts in a journal, focusing on how these insights can guide you as you embrace the spirit of service in your recovery journey. By reflecting on this spread, you can find deeper meaning in your commitment to helping others while continuing to nurture your own healing.

A RITUAL TO BE OF SERVICE THROUGH A SPIRITUAL AWAKENING

— ◇ —

This is a ritual to embody the spirit of service, share your journey, and promote healing for yourself and others. The essence of this act is to embrace service, connection, and the strength gained from your spiritual awakening.

Materials Needed

White candle (for purity and spiritual awakening) and a means to light it

Oil for anointing the candle (olive and sunflower are great options, but anything that resonates for you will work)

Herbs (like sage or rosemary for cleansing or lavender for peace)

Piece of paper and pen (to write your commitments or messages)

Small bowl of water (as a symbol of emotional healing)

Crystals like clear quartz (for clarity) or amethyst (for sobriety and spiritual growth) (optional)

The Spell

+ Cleanse your energy as well as the energy around your Sobriety Altar. Set your intentions by taking a moment to reflect on your journey through sobriety and your desire to help others. Decide what specific commitment you want to make regarding service or sharing your experience.

+ If your candle is a freestanding taper, anoint it with a bit of oil, just enough to make it slightly tacky. Run the oil onto the candle before rolling it in the herbs or gently pressing them onto the surface so they stick to the candle. If your candle is in a jar, you may sprinkle the herbs around the base instead.

+ As you light the candle, say this affirmation out loud: "With this flame, I seek clarity and understanding. I commit to sharing my journey with others, bringing light to those in darkness."

+ On the piece of paper, write down your intention or a message you wish to convey to those struggling with addiction. This could be a quote, a personal insight, or an affirmation of support.

+ Dip your fingers in the bowl of water, visualizing it as a source of healing. As you do so, say: "May this water cleanse my spirit and serve as a reminder of the healing I seek for myself and others."

+ Fold the paper with your commitment and hold it in your hands. Focus on sending your energy and intention into it, and say out loud: "I offer my strength and experience as a beacon of hope. May my words reach those who need them."

+ Spend a few minutes in quiet meditation. Visualize yourself sharing your story and helping others find their path to recovery. Imagine the positive impact you can have radiating outward like a spiderweb of healing threads imbued with love.

+ When you feel ready, thank your higher power and any deities or spirits that you feel guided to acknowledge and extinguish the candle. Do this with gratitude for the support you've received in your journey.

After the ritual, take some time to reflect on your experience. Journal about any feelings or insights that came up during the process, and remind yourself of your commitment to service. Make a plan to carry out your commitment, whether that's volunteering, sharing your story in a meeting, or simply reaching out to someone in need.

CONCLUSION
THE JOURNEY CONTINUES

So we've drawn every card in the Major Arcana and come to the end! But of course the end isn't ever *really* the end ...

The Fool's Journey isn't a straight path: it's a cycle—always turning, always evolving, just like the journey of sobriety and healing. Every time we think we've "arrived," life throws us back into a new adventure, a new lesson, a new leap of faith. The Fool starts out wide-eyed and fearless, stepping into the unknown. As they move through the cards, they face challenges, growth, and moments of deep transformation. And by the time they reach the World, there's a sense of completion ... but not finality. Just like in life, every ending is another beginning. We're always stepping off a cliff into something new, carrying the wisdom of our past journeys with us.

This Fool's Journey is never truly over either. Recovery, like witchcraft and tarot, is a lifelong practice of trust, surrender, intention, and transformation. We begin as seekers, stepping into the unknown, and along the way, we gather wisdom, face our shadows, and learn what it truly means to heal. And just when we think we've reached the end, life invites us to start again.

Sobriety has taught me that healing isn't about reaching some perfect state of being—it's about showing up, over and over, for the work of growth and self-discovery. Witchcraft has taught me that I have power and can weave my intentions into the fabric of my life and shape my own path. Tarot has shown me that every experience—joy, pain, loss, renewal—has meaning, that every card pulled is part of a greater story. And the twelve steps have shown me that surrender isn't weakness—it's freedom. I am now working *with* the Universe instead of fighting against it.

There are so many reasons why substances can feel like the solution to help us cope—to numb ourselves, to deal with our highly sensitive natures, to dull our triggers. Eliminating alcohol doesn't take all our problems away, but a sober lifestyle empowers us to understand our motivations, consider different choices, and mindfully create supportive, beneficial solutions rather than causing chaos and making situations worse. It's OK to feel a lot. It's good to be a fool and take chances and try new things and get into situations beyond our comfort zones. Through recovery, we can ride out that discomfort and create meaningful changes so we can enjoy our lives fully present and in brilliant Technicolor!

I hope this book has reconnected you to your own power—because it's always been there within you. You get to use that power however you wish, and you get to decide what's right for *you*. As new challenges come up, you can turn to these spells, rituals, and card spreads whenever you need them. Just like the tarot cards you pull don't appear in numerical order, the tools in this book aren't a methodical routine for you to follow; they're meant to support you whenever they are most helpful. And I want you to make this practice your own. Spells and rituals aren't meant to be followed word for word—they're here to inspire you, to spark something within you. Change them, adapt them, weave in your own magic. Experiment, play, and embody the Fool by taking chances and trying new things. Trust your intuition because your path is yours alone. What matters isn't how perfectly you follow a ritual but the energy and intention you bring to it.

If there's one thing I hope you take from this book, it's that you are both the reader and the writer of your own story. The cards don't tell us what to do; they hold up a mirror, offering insight, possibility, and choice. Witchcraft and tarot don't hand us easy answers; they teach us to work with energy, with nature, and with spirit—as well as to trust ourselves. And recovery doesn't promise a perfect life; instead, it offers us a path to walk, one day at a time, with honesty and grace.

Whether you are just beginning or years into sobriety, know this: You are not alone. You are capable of transformation, of healing, of reclaiming your own magic. The magic is already inside you. The wisdom is already within reach. It's been an honor to take this journey with you. The path is now yours to walk, and when you step forward, even when you don't know exactly where you're going, the Universe will meet you there.

Take that step into the unknown. Trust the journey. The Fool always finds their way.

ADDITIONAL READING

These are a few of the books that had a profound impact on me during my first year of sobriety.

Women Who Run with the Wolves
by Clarissa Pinkola Estes, PhD

If you're having a mental breakdown or have hit rock bottom, this is a crucial read providing a powerful exploration of the human spirit and resiliency through myths and stories of inner strength and intuition. This book reminded me that suffering is a shared aspect of the human experience, but so is redemption: we can go through the darkness of hard times and emerge on the other side guided by the light of our inner spark. It's also a wonderful thing to be wild and not feel the need to always tame yourself.

All About Love
by bell hooks

This should be required reading for everyone, as hooks provides a profoundly helpful perspective on the complexities of love as not just a feeling but an action with the transformative power to create societal change and the radical importance of showing love to ourselves.

Seventy-Eight Degrees of Wisdom
by Rachel Pollack

This is the most thorough and complete book on tarot written by an icon in the field. If you are interested in going further with tarot, this is essential for your collection. Rachel's message is positive as she reminds readers that even difficult life experiences offer potential for transformative growth.

Power of the Witch
by Laurie Cabot

Sobriety offered me an opportunity to reconnect to stuff I loved when I was younger, including this book, which was a favorite of mine as a baby witch. Laurie is a profound elder of the craft, and her story of finding her power has always inspired me. She also offers wonderful, easily applicable tips on how to bring magical practices into your everyday life.

ACKNOWLEDGMENTS

This book would not exist without the love, encouragement, and gentle pushes from the people who've walked alongside me through the most magical and most uncertain moments of my life. Thank you for believing in me when I didn't always believe in myself, for reminding me of the power of my voice, and for holding space while I found my way home to it. The opposite of addiction isn't just sobriety; it's connection and community. There is magic in knowing we don't have to do it alone, and this book is a reminder of that.

To my parents, Amy and Ralph and Steve and Kathy, thank you for always supporting my creativity. Your love gave me the foundation to explore, to imagine, and to make my dreams come true.

To my editor, Shannon Kelly, thank you for understanding the heart of my vision and helping me shape it with so much care. I am endlessly grateful for your insight, support, and encouragement. You truly manifested our connection through your Post-it note spell!

To my agent, Tom Flannery, thank you for seeing the magic in this project and in me. You understood my vision from the beginning and your faith in this concept made all the difference.

To the entire team at Running Press, thank you for embracing my story and helping me bring it to life. You have all made this collaborative process feel so joyful!

To Lisa Stardust, my cosmic sister, this book wouldn't exist without your support! Thank you for your unwavering encouragement, your friendship, and your magic.

To Alee Hoffman, who literally saw this book waiting for me in the Akashic records before I even had the language for it. Thank you for holding that vision until I was ready to walk into it.

To Anka Lavriv, whose friendship reminds me that the universe is always conspiring in our favor. You arrived in my life at exactly the right moment, a living reminder of the magic of divine timing.

To Erik Foss who showed me that sobriety is wildly fun and dreams really do come true in the most magical city in the world, NYC!

To all of my friends who are more like chosen family, Kellesimone Waits, Alice Steinmetz, Victoria Meyer, Kelsey Bennett, Daniel Rosenblum, Jan Pappas, David Hurwitz, Zac Clark, Molly Kraus, Annakim Violette, Amanda Mossing, Janet Schnol, Hillary Weinstein Rivman, and the beloveds who walk beside me, you held me through deadlines, heartbreaks, and spells that took their sweet time to work. Thank you for the laughter, the pep talks, the late-night texts, and for never letting me give up on myself or this book.

To my mentor LeeAnn, thank you for guiding me through the realms of intuition with so much grace, clarity, and generosity. Your mentorship deepened my trust in my psychic gifts and reminded me of the sacred responsibility that comes with them.

To the recovery communities that have saved my life again and again, thank you for showing me how to surrender, how to stay, how to live fearlessly with truth, and how to begin again. You are in every page.

To the ones who book readings, come to my ceremonies, whisper your wishes into the moonlight with me, who set intentions with me and share the joy of dreams finally coming true, thank you. Your courage and vulnerability continue to inspire me. You remind me that magic is real, and it's happening right here, right now.

To the witches and weirdos, the sensitives and seekers, the ones navigating healing, grief, and glitter, this book is for you. It's wonderful to feel everything deeply because being tuned in and compassionate are superpowers.

And to the moon and stars, Venus, Iris, Polly Styrene, and my inner teen, my most abundant sources of inspiration and greatest muses! Thank you for guiding me through this lifetime.

ABOUT THE AUTHOR

SARAH POTTER is a professional witch, intuitive tarot reader, and magical educator based in New York City. A lifelong practitioner and voice in the modern mystic movement, she blends spirituality, ritual, and personal transformation to help others find their magic on a path rooted in joy, intuition, and radical self-trust.